dilemma     training

# Am I Right?
## – Or –
# Am I Right?

**An introduction to ethical decision making**

# Simon Geschwindt

Order this book online at www.trafford.com
or email orders@trafford.com

Most Trafford titles are also available at major online book retailers.

First Published in Britain 2006
Simon Geschwindt has asserted his right under Britain's Copyright, Designs and Patents Act 1988
to be identified as the author of this work.

| Illustrations: | Joey Carroll. |
| Photos: | Christian Schnell, Hannover, Germany. |
| | Istockphotos, Calgary, Canada. |
| Cover design: | Joey Carroll and Simon Geschwindt. |

Note for Librarians: A cataloguing record for this book is available from Library
and Archives Canada at www.collectionscanada.ca/amicus/index-e.html

Printed in Victoria, BC, Canada.

ISBN: 978-1-4251-1926-3

*Our mission is to efficiently provide the world's finest, most comprehensive
book publishing service, enabling every author to experience success.
To find out how to publish your book, your way, and have it available
worldwide, visit us online at www.trafford.com/*

 www.trafford.com

**North America & international**
toll-free: 1 888 232 4444 (USA & Canada)
phone: 250 383 6864 ♦ fax: 812 355 4082

# DEDICATION

*This book is dedicated to my wife Karin, children Maarten, Maaike, Tim, Siôn and Liam, my parents Hermann and Alice Geschwindt, and – 'all the beaten and butchered and betrayed and martyred children of the earth'.*

## ACKNOWLEDGEMENTS

I would like to thank my good friends and colleagues, Joanna Haynes and Karin Murris, for their inspiration and significant contributions to the chapters on Animal Rights, and Freedom, and sections headed *What is the 'environment'?*, *Vive la différence*, and *Is it right to punish?* and Karin's chapter on Education. I would also like to thank Ian Ground at the University of Sunderland for his contribution to the introduction to the chapter on Business, and Dr Trevor Curnow of St Martin's College, University of Lancashire for his help with the chapter on Tobacco.

# THE AUTHOR

Simon Geschwindt is a freelance journalist specializing in business ethics and the environment. Simon holds a BA (Hons) in humanities, majoring in Philosophy of Art and Ethics, and has undertaken postgraduate study in Ethics and eastern philosophies. He worked for many years as a Benelux correspondent for *Financial Times Business Information* (FTBI) before moving to Britain as an energy markets editor for *La Tribune* and *L'Agence Economique et Financière* (L'AGEFI) in Paris. He was managing editor of the international publication, *Environment Matters*, before joining UK ethics consultancy, Dialogue Works, as Head of Communications. He is author of the novel *Lost Identity*. Simon, born 1949, is married with five children, and lives in Johannesburg.

*'At Auschwitz, tell me, where was God?'*
*And the answer: 'Where was man?'*
*Sophie's Choice by William Styron*

# CONTENTS

# PREFACE

This book was written at the start of 2005, against a backdrop of commemoration of the end of one of the worst acts of evil ever known, and two displays of selfless charity by ordinary people on an unprecedented scale.

Appeals for help for the victims of the *Tsunami* tidal wave that ravaged parts of Sri Lanka and Southeast Asia raised hundreds of millions of pounds from Britain alone, from people who had no personal connection with the victims. Later in the year saw the *Live8* concerts to raise funds to beat African poverty.

Such generosity of spirit was in stark contrast to the dark period of Europe's history marked by worldwide commemoration of the 60th anniversary of the end of World War Two and the liberation of Auschwitz concentration camp by the Red Army. Sixty years ago world leaders vowed that it must never happen again.

There has been no 'World War Three', but there has been a world full of wars. And the horrors of the holocaust *have* happened again and again – in the form of persecution of intellectuals, religious intolerance, genocide, ethnic cleansing and neo imperialism.

There appears to be no 'final solution' to the intolerance people show towards those who are different, who are 'strangers'.

In 2005 there was peace throughout Europe resting precariously on an unprecedented economic interdependence. Yet, conservative political parties were already appealing to a xenophobic return to nationhood, and a distancing from the European Union.

If Europe is to continue to be a more peaceful place, and the rest of the world has a chance of catching up, it is vital that today's children – tomorrow's adults – are able to make the right decisions and are empowered to 'think for themselves' and to take accounts of others.

This book provides you with the opportunity to think about the ways in which the choices you make matter to yourself and others. The aim is not to provide you with an off-the-peg theory for self-development. Rather, it is to help you appreciate the habit of *thinking for yourself* before you act, or at the very least to be able to justify your actions after the event.

By emphasising the need for personal responsibility in ethical decision making this book does not intend to be anti-authority *per se* – nor anti-religion. There are good laws, for example, but also bad laws. There is good religious doctrine, but also bad or misleading dogma. This in no way impinges upon the way religions can add a spiritual dimension and meaning to people's lives. It simply stresses that, perhaps after consulting a relevant authority, you should always ask yourself 'is what I am about to do morally right?'

To help you answer that question, this book introduces you to *Dilemma Training* – a relatively straightforward programme of ethical decision making, and one that acknowledges that ethical behaviour rests largely on tolerance and empathy for others and respect for their beliefs, desires and ways of life.

The *Dilemma Training* mantra is 'Think for yourself' – ask yourself 'is what I am doing morally right?' Justifying actions by appealing to authorities is a betrayal. 'I was only obeying orders', 'Everyone does it', 'I had no choice', 'My religion dictates it', 'It's a tradition', 'It's always been like that' are not ethical reasons. They are excuses.

The aim of this book is to encourage you to face the world as it really is, not as you might wish it to be. We might think it would be nicer if the kinds of dilemmas which this book is about could be relegated to a separate, isolated realm, kept well away from the motivations, choices and outcomes that make up everyday life. It might be more comfortable – for a while. But, like ignoring debts, one day there will be a knock at the door.

Ethical decision making is not a leisure interest for armchair philosophers or dinner-party chat for middle class sophisticates. It needs to be an integral part of life for all of us – an integral part of *integrity*.

**Part I** of the book introduces the concept of ethical decision making, and examines the notion of integrity. It goes on to explain the various moral theories and the relevance of stakeholder interests in making ethical decisions, as well as providing an insight into the tools necessary for decision making.

**Part II** describes *Dilemma Training* in action. Starting with education and substance abuse, it focuses mainly on the dilemmas faced by children, youngsters and those who deal with them such as teachers, parents, youth workers and the police. Children hopefully become adults, and the book moves on to deal with dilemmas faced by those in 'grown up' areas such as local government, business, the armed forces and the media.

**Part III** discusses the ethical elements of some 'big issues': environment, science, animals, race, the workplace, capital punishment, euthanasia and suicide.

**Part IV** gives examples of ethical dilemmas from literature, and summarises the historical development of 'thinking for yourself' with emphasis on the role of religion.

Past guidance on moral issues has derived mainly from theology and philosophy. Although this book rests largely on moral philosophy, it has not been written with the scholarly rigour associated with the subject. It is not aimed at philosophers and theologians, but is written by an everyday person for everyday people who need to resolve difficult choices between what seem to be conflicting right courses of action. However, there are numerous references to philosophers whose thinking informs the history of ethical decision making and the various schools of thought on the subject.

One glaring absence is that of bioethics – ethical decision making in the health care professions. This is because the subject is already highly developed, and has been extensively covered elsewhere. The exceptions are the chapters covering euthanasia and suicide where the dilemmas are mainly personal rather than the sole province of health care professionals.

You can read this book from cover to cover, or you can skip to chapters that you can see are relevant to your domestic or professional situation, or the types of dilemmas you are likely to be faced with. However, *Part I* is essential reading.

I WAS SURPRISED AT HOW EASILY THEY PERSUADED ME TO THINK FOR MYSELF.

# PART I

# 1

# AM I RIGHT? OR AM I RIGHT?

In the novel *Sophie's Choice* by William Styron, Sophie is transported to Auschwitz with her two small children. Upon her arrival an inebriated SS doctor tells Sophie she can take only one of her children with her into the camp and that the other one will go to the ovens. The power-crazed doctor screams at her that if she doesn't pick one, she will lose them both. How can she choose?

She has seconds in which to decide. In such circumstances how can any choice be ethically justified?

Thankfully, dilemmas in life are hardly ever as brutally stark as this – and rarely are the stakes so high. Yet the ability to make the right choices in any dilemma is fundamental to a good life. And making the effort to work out the right choice should make it a lot easier to live with. Knowing how to do the right thing is an essential part of the tool kit with which to maintain an authentic and autonomous existence.

Sophie didn't have that part of the tool kit. She acted on instinct – a gut reaction. And whether or not they turn out to produce the 'right' decisions, gut reactions tend to be difficult to justify ethically after the event. Sophie survives Auschwitz. She knows one of her children is dead, and she never sees the other again. In the author's words, the two of them have joined the other 'beaten and butchered and betrayed and martyred children of the earth'.

**Insurance against guilt**

If you have the opportunity and knowledge to systemati-cally and rationally think through your choices, that choice is surely a lot easier to live with long after the event.

Sophie is haunted by the thought that she might have made a series of wrong choices that ultimately led to a disastrously wrong choice in Auschwitz. 'What if...?' questions torment her for the rest of her short life. After moving to the States she drifts through life aimlessly. Her lovely smile, switched on and off for the sake of social acceptance, masks a deep-rooted depression. 'Her guilt is murdering her just as surely as her children were murdered...'

Sophie's choice is not an everyday ethical dilemma, but it is a particularly striking one because of the barren environment within which it takes place – an environment where all morality and human goodness have been structurally abandoned.

Hers is not only one of the most awful choices imaginable, it consists of two choices – the choice of which child should go to the gas chamber, and the choice to make such a choice. Her choices are brutally forced upon her in an environment so extreme, and where the stakes are so high, that decisions are stripped bare of any of the usual safety nets. If you can uphold your integrity in Auschwitz, you can uphold it anywhere.

Also, Sophie herself, apart from her stunning beauty, is really quite ordinary. She is no superwoman, no heroine, just an everyday person. Her actions and reactions are probably typical of anyone in her position. Yet had she had the opportunity and knowledge to systematically and rationally think through her choice, that choice would surely have been easier to live with.

# Like a house on fire

*'Sooner or later one has to take sides. If one is to remain human.'*

Mr Heng, in The Quiet American, Graham Greene, 1955.

Would Sophie's choice have been easier if, rather than choosing between her two children, she had been forced to choose between her child and, for example, her mother, brother or lover? Would it have been easier if her little girl had been a Down's syndrome child?

There is a thought experiment known as the *burning house*. Imagine you come home one day to find your house on fire. At one top floor window your young child is screaming for help. At another window your elderly parents are crying out to be rescued from the flames. You know you have only enough time to get a ladder up to one of the windows. Which one will it be?

There is no time for utilitarian-style calculations such as weighing up the benefits of one child's life measured against that of two elderly people. You have to decide in a matter of seconds. But how?

Try the same thought experiment with others at the windows. Try for example your brother and sister at one window, and your parents at the other. Then imagine any others you can think of.

| Left window | Right window |
|---|---|
| My brother | My workmates |
| My boss | My local publican |
| My neighbours | Some foreign tourists |
| A policeman | A known thief |

Thought experiments are a useful yardstick with which to measure your likely decisions in certain circumstances – to give a clue to your probable decision making. But they offer little insight into the morality of those decisions – your *ethical* decision making. For that you need to consider the 'ethics' underlying the action.

# 2

## DEFINE YOUR TERMS

**What do we mean by 'ethics'?**

---

*'I shall tell you a great secret, my friend. Do not wait for the last judgement. It takes place every day.'*

*Albert Camus, 1913-60, from La Chute (The Fall) 1956.*

---

Ethics concerns action – right or wrong action. There are two senses of 'ethics' – the everyday sense and how it is used by professional ethicists and philosophers. Usually, ethics refers to specific moral values that govern conduct. When you talk about the ethics of our politicians, you refer to the types of moral decisions that they make and the kinds of attitudes and ideas which lead them to make those decisions.

For the professional philosopher, ethics is a branch of philosophical enquiry like philosophy of religion or of art. It refers to the systematic study of the nature of moral thinking. As an intellectual enquiry, it is not necessarily concerned with particular practical issues concerning right or wrong, but is a study of moral theory.

The two senses of 'ethics' are intertwined. Philosophers often argue for particular moral views about particular moral issues. And, perhaps more importantly, people who aren't professional philosophers do reflect systematically on their own personal ethical codes and the ethics of those around them.

Your own individual ethics does not have to involve commitment to any particular ethical theory. Making ethical decisions is not just an intellectual affair but also involves your emotions. You need to be compassionate, sympathetic and engaged just as much as you need to be consistent, objective and detached.

Rather than regarding what you morally *think* as something quite separable from what you morally *feel*, it would be better to think of your moral feelings as underpinning your moral thought. This is true of positive emotions such as compassion and generosity, but unfortunately it is also true of less admirable ones such as fear and envy. The sort of feelings that will determine how you act will depend on your *integrity*.

**What do we mean by 'integrity'?**

It is often said that integrity is all or nothing, that you can't have a little integrity. One problem of this 'either/or' approach is that you never know quite at what stage of your self-development you've finally 'got it'. It's much more useful to regard integrity as something acquired and developed on a long path of consistently – wherever and whenever – trying to apply ethical decision making to your conscious choices, in accordance with your core values, rather than merely for the sake of expediency.

Whatever crises and pressures rain down upon you, your integrity depends on your keeping your moral head 'while all about you are losing theirs', to quote Kipling's *If*. You try not to be duplicitous, and you are therefore trusted, because those around you know what you stand for – what they see is what they get.

People with integrity use skills such as being careful, prudent, diligent, vigilant, deliberate, and they have a sense of what is material and important. It is typical of people with integrity that they are strong, and that they find some way of overcoming fear and disappointment and not backing down. Their belief in the rightness of their actions gives them the confidence to meet major challenges, knowing that they have the capabilities and skills to deal effectively with the situation at hand.

Integrity should not translate into a moral crusade. Integrity implies taking account of the rights, desires and needs of others. There is no place for intolerance.

People with integrity often have the approval of others. They include those who know what to do – 'a good man in a crisis' – who are reliable. But approval is not a sufficient condition of having integrity. Another trait that is frequently admired is ruthlessness when the occasion demands it – an exhibition of strength. Another is people who do what they say they're going to do – even when it's not ethical!

But this kind of consistency is not a *sufficient* condition of having integrity. Mild-mannered, happily-married, Catholic, Auschwitz Kommandant, Rudolf Höss, was consistently a man of duty and could be relied upon by his friends, family, and colleagues, including the architect of the *Final Solution*, Heinrich Himmler. He performed his duties with ruthlessness, and was also kind to animals and a loving father. (For 'necessary and sufficient conditions' see Chapter 7.)

There is a crucial deficiency that explains Höss' lack of real integrity. It was the ethical dimension in relation to the SS circle of stakeholders and a complete lack of empathy for people outside that circle that were the vital elements missing from his moral make-up. Although his memoirs claim otherwise, he appeared to show no tolerance, empathy or respect for the rights and wishes of those outside the SS circle.

# Circles of concern – the stakeholders

**Circles of concern – the stakeholders**

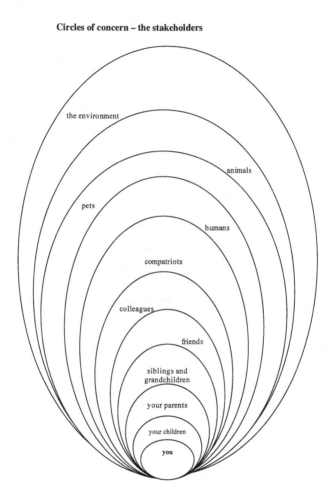

## What are virtues?

Integrity – completeness – is not itself a virtue but the *integration* of a whole gamut of virtues. It is linked to character. Acting with integrity is a form of skilled behaviour. It is not sufficient to hold a moral belief or value if you do not have the skills and information with which to successfully apply it.

Being human means you have the capacity to reflect on your own actions – a capacity which, as far as we know, is denied members of other species. But that capacity is also denied certain members of the human species – for example, babies and young infants, the mentally ill and the demented. Where precisely can we place the notion of personal responsibility and that of diminished responsibility?

A virtue denotes a disposition to act in certain ways. Being virtuous means *consistently* behaving in accordance with certain core values such as courage, fairness, honesty, justice, kindness, loyalty, patience, and so on.

That also applies to organisations. A group's core values are those that have been agreed by its members and apply to each member, as well as to the group as a whole.

Integrity is also about self-restraint – not always doing what you feel like doing, but about doing what you believe is right, where you can answer positively the question 'is what I am doing morally right?'

However, a disposition to act virtuously is not necessarily enough. You have to be free to do so. It must be reasonably possible to act virtuously. Your integrity reflects how you act freely in the same *real* circumstances under the same *real* pressures.

Freedom is crucial. It could be argued that Sophie's choice is not a choice at all – that the SS doctor gives her only the cruel illusion of choice. A real choice depends on its being made by someone who has complete freedom of choice.

However, complete freedom of choice is more or less theoretical. Most real-life dilemmas involve choices in circumstances that are anything but 'free'. Perhaps the answer is that there is no answer. There are rarely perfectly good or bad choices. They are only good or bad by degree.

## What are values?

Values are personal judgements that determine how you actually behave. Most values, such as the belief in the right to a roof over your head, have nothing to do with ethics. They are relevant to ethics only when they are based on beliefs about what is right – such as that it is right to take account of others involved – even the rights of non-humans such as animals or the environment where appropriate.

Values are usually based on religious beliefs, cultural tradition, family background, personal experiences, laws and professional conduct. The values that underpin the best ethical decisions are those that are independent of these influences, are carefully thought out and are universal. They include such values as trustworthiness, respect, responsibility and fairness. They are applicable to everyone, everywhere, always.

Values often conflict. For example, your desire to be honest may clash with the desire to be loyal. In such cases, you need to consult your value system, and the *Dilemma Training* method is eminently suited to doing this.

The values you consistently rank higher than others are your core values. You apply your core values to ethical principles, which become your rules of conduct.

*Dilemma Training* does not prescribe ethical decision making based on certain values. What it does do is enable you to formulate more easily your core values, so that you can understand decisions better – your own decisions and those of others.

For example, one of the most important, if not *the* most important, core value is 'honesty'. Honesty implies truthfulness – not the truth necessarily, but telling what you believe to be true. It excludes the sort of white lies, half-truths, rhetorical devices and even 'no comments' that are meant to mislead.

Yet, even this ethical cornerstone is not inviolate. Occasionally, dishonesty is ethically justifiable, as when loyalty overrides truth telling. But such occasions are rare and should be reserved for very serious situations – not matters of life and death necessarily, but certainly not, for example, for expediency or merely to avoid a confrontation or embarrassment.

Another value, linked to honesty, is promise keeping. When someone is counting on something you have promised, you have a moral duty to that person to keep your promise. You also have a duty to make sure you make only promises you can keep – and that all parties to it understand what's involved.

**Integrity – who needs it?**

---

*'Integrity without knowledge is weak and useless, and knowledge without integrity is dangerous and dreadful.'*

*Samuel Johnson, 1709-1784.*

---

Now that we have some idea of what integrity is, the next question is why bother with it? Beyond the concerns of your immediate family, such as in Sophie's choice, why bother trying to make your choices ethical? If 'One man's profit is another man's loss', it makes sense to be the man with the profit. Why worry about the man with the loss? Why should you 'Do unto others as you would have done unto yourself'? If you're fit, strong and have the right kind of friends, why not live by the motto 'might is right'. If other people don't serve your own self-interest, why not, in the words of Mario Puzo's *Godfather*, 'make them an offer they can't refuse'.

Unless you are an irredeemable psychopath, there are several reasons you should bother with integrity, why it's good to be good. Some are virtuous; some are not.

There can be a personal advantage. In the long run it's prudent to be ethical. It's good for business. And being ethical boosts self-esteem, and earns you the respect of family, friends and peers. But this sounds like pure self-interest. Not that there's anything wrong with self-interest. But once it becomes the sole motivation, decision making degenerates into a series of cost-benefit calculations. When that happens, in cases where the risks of ethical behaviour are high – or the risks from unethical behaviour are low and the rewards are high – ethics capitulates to expediency.

The acid test is whether you stick to your beliefs about the right course of action, even when it's not in your self-interest. But again – why bother?

One assumption is that your conscience bothers you if you don't, and that a bad conscience will make you unhappy. Basically, conscience is the awareness of the moral aspect of how you behave; it nags you (hopefully) to prefer right to wrong. But this assumes you have a conscience. After all, people with no conscience who act badly feel just as good about themselves as someone acting well but with a clear conscience.

Apart from appealing to your conscience, what other reasons are there for being ethical, particularly in an age when there are no religious sanctions for bad behaviour? Why not drive like a maniac through a village, putting kids' and old ladies' lives in jeopardy, and brake to the speed limit only a few metres away from the speed camera?

There are other reasons. One is that acting with integrity is likely to make you happier. Of course this depends on how you define happiness. And this depends on your values.

Whether having integrity makes you happy can also depend on your own attitude towards integrity, happiness and life in general. As the Prussian philosopher Arthur Schopenhauer famously and miserably pointed out, fulfilment of desires rarely leads to lasting happiness. They more often lead to repeated waves of dissatisfaction.

There is a dichotomy between 'desire' and 'pleasure'. It has been asserted that the part of the brain associated with desire is quite separate from the part of the brain associated with pleasure, and that fulfilling desire – not just material but any kind of desire, such as wanting to read a book or understand a theory, will not necessarily provide pleasure, and that a lot of things that have nothing to do with desire, such as the delight of seeing children playing, the year's first bluebells or an unexpected gift can be profound sources of pleasure. Desire and pleasure can be completely separate.

Fulfilment of the desire to be a person of integrity, therefore, will not necessarily make you happy. But it is more likely that your spontaneous 'good' acts – acts of kindness and generosity, being a *mensch*, a decent, upright, mature, and responsible person, the kind of person people can always count on – will provide the kind of pleasure that can lead to happiness.

For most people, it's nicer to be liked than disliked. That might be at the expense of being disliked by those who lack integrity – being regarded as a 'goody two shoes' – but who needs their approval anyway?

# I wouldn't be seen dead...

*'Conscience is the inner voice which warns us that someone may be looking.'*

H L Mencken, 1880-1956.

If God is not watching you, and you don't care a jot about your neighbours' opinion of you, and you don't believe in karma and reincarnation, and you're indifferent towards being liked or disliked, then what is there to stop you from behaving badly?

Perhaps you do care about what you will bequeath to those you will leave behind. Because 'you know not the time nor the place', and because all that will remain of you after you've passed on is other people's memory of you, whatever you were doing at the moment of your death could be of considerable significance.

This leads to a useful ethical maxim: *never do what you wouldn't want to be seen dead having done.* Reflection upon this important maxim can significantly strengthen your integrity.

Nonetheless, all this still boils down to self-interest, albeit obliquely. All you can safely conclude is that the key to the value of ethical decision making is that it promotes self-interest while at the same time allowing for the interests and rights of others – of the stakeholders – and from the standpoint of all concerned, that has to be significantly superior to acting solely according to self-interest.

## Can integrity be taught?

Can integrity be taught? The short answer is 'no'. But it can be acquired, and the skills necessary to acquiring it can be taught or, more to the point, can be learned.

So how do you find the knowledge to systematically and rationally think through ethical decisions, assuming you've got enough time? There is no magic bullet. Nonetheless, training in decision making can provide a tool to help you to do the right thing, and using it regularly can help you make the right decisions even when time is short and you are under extreme pressure. It's a bit like physical training – the more you do it, the faster and sharper you become.

# 3

## DO UNTO OTHERS...

*'There is nothing abstract or idealistic about the call to love your neighbour.'*

The Right Reverend Rowan Williams, Archbishop of Canterbury, July 2005, ahead of the G8 summit in Scotland.

*'Do not do unto others as you would that they should do unto you. Their tastes may not be the same.'*

George Bernard Shaw, Man and Superman, 1903.

Having established that a key to the value of ethical decision making is that it promotes self-interest while at the same time allowing for the interests and rights of others, you need to establish who these 'others' are.

All those affected by a decision have a stake in that decision – they are the stakeholders. And, as such, they have a resultant moral claim on the decision maker. Ethical decisions take into account the possible consequences for all those potentially affected.

Such decision making necessitates systematic and disciplined assessment of whom a decision could affect, as well as considerate care about the way it could affect others. This outlaws manipulation and exploitation of others, and reflects notions such as autonomy, dignity and tolerance. Through *Dilemma Training* you practise assessing possible consequences and taking reasonable steps to avoid hurting others.

To effectively pinpoint the stakeholders affected by your choice of action demands a certain amount of *empathy* – putting yourself in their shoes. Empathy in turn rests largely on *imagination* – to enable you to imagine what it is like to be in another's shoes.

In *Dilemma Training* you learn to deal with situations where upholding one moral principle would mean sacrificing another – where, for example, you tell the truth while ignoring the duty to be loyal, or where demands for loyalties produce a conflict of interest.

We all share a duty in principle to care for and respect others. But this can move one step further into the realm of 'loyalty'. What do we mean by 'loyalty'? Loyalty is a responsibility to promote the interests of certain people or organisations.

**Who are the 'others'? – prioritising loyalties**

So many people and organisations can claim your loyalty that you need to prioritise them. For example, it is perfectly reasonable, and ethical, to look after the interests of your own children, and that this overrides any concern for other people's children. The 'burning house' thought experiment is extremely useful in deciding how to rank your priorities.

On the other hand, we all owe a duty of care for the planet – not that we are powerful enough to destroy it, but we are capable of ruining it as a viable habitat for the human species. Its survival as a habitat is essential to the continued existence of billions of people. Yet it is highly unlikely that any mother would sacrifice the life of her child for the sake of saving the planet. Some might say that compared with a mother's duty to her child, her duty to the planet is too remote – not in her backyard. Yet this seems at first sight to be patently absurd. Her backyard is part of the planet. Yet the argument is perfectly sound when judged in terms of *emotional* proximity or remoteness.

In the wider circles of stakeholders, can there be a duty to people you will never even meet?

In December 2004 the *Tsunami* tidal wave hit Indonesia, Sri Lanka, India, Somalia, Thailand, Maldives, and other countries, causing huge loss of life and massive material devastation.

Against those that argue that an absence of religion produces an absence of care and altruism, the people of Britain – one of the most secular countries in the world – were extremely generous in their response to the crisis, and in their sympathy for the *Tsunami* victims who were far outside their immediate circles of interest.

In terms of the circles of stakeholders there might be a tenuous link with the people of the former British colonies, but British people have absolutely no connection at all with the people of other parts of the world that were hit by the tidal wave such as Muslims in Indonesia, apart from the fact that they were fellow humans.

### Live8 – Extending the circles

*'While there is poverty there is no freedom. We know what to do and we know what it will cost. We now need leadership, vision and political courage.'*

*Nelson Mandela, Live8, Johannesburg, July 2005.*

In July 2005, the leaders of the world's eight most powerful nations gathered in Scotland for the G8 summit, and were presented with a workable plan to double aid to less developed countries, drop their debt to western banks, and make the trade laws fairer to poor countries. This was preceded by *Live8*, organised by Irish rockstar Sir Bob Geldof. It consisted of 10 concerts, 100 artists, one million spectators, two billion viewers, and one message: to get those eight men, in that one room, to stop 30,000 children dying every single day of extreme poverty.

At the *Live8* concert in Johannesburg former South African

president, Nelson Mandela, called upon the world leaders meeting at the G8 summit in Scotland to take action to relieve poverty.

That fragile man well into his eighties looked as if he could have been puffed away by the slightest breeze. The emotional restraint with which he made his plea to the leaders of the world's richest nations had the power that comes from feelings so deep that the emotions associated with them leave the outward appearance undisturbed.

His speech was followed by a similarly restrained and moving performance by Pink Floyd. The banner behind the band said it all: **NO MORE EXCUSES!**

# 4

# EXCUSES, EXCUSES

*'Whoever in debate quotes authority uses not intellect, but memory.'*

*Leonardo Da Vinci, 1452-1519*

Sometimes you might feel powerless to make the right decisions. Outside pressures such as conflicting loyalties, lack of time or even exhaustion may completely undermine your ability to make a decision at all, let alone ethically. The same can be said of negative reactions, such as those coupled with emotions such as anger, fear, and jealousy.

On top of that, you need to be on guard against a myriad of potential obstacles, in the form of rationalisations and excuses. Rationalisation and wishful thinking form a veil between you and the truth.

The law, for example is not alone sufficient to underpin ethical decisions. Many laws are good; many are not. An action that is allowed under the law or a particular code of conduct can still be immoral. The torture and murder of the inmates of Auschwitz was perfectly legal under the German law that prevailed in occupied territories such as Poland during the early 1940s. Ill-treatment of suspected 'terrorists' is currently legal under American law, as is capital punishment.

In all cases and circumstances, whatever the law prescribes or whatever the received wisdom, to act authentically and with integrity means being guided primarily by your core values, and accepting responsibility for your own ethical decisions.

The excuse offered by a US military police officer to justify her involvement in ill-treatment of prisoners in Iraq's Abu

Ghraib prison was that she was only obeying orders. In most cases justifying actions by appealing to authorities is a betrayal of personal responsibility and autonomy.

'My religion dictates it' was one of the excuses exploited for decades by the white minority in South Africa to excuse *apartheid*, and is used to justify religious fundamentalist crime in the East and in the West.

Many otherwise perfectly decent people believe that ethical standards at work are different from those at home or in other realms of life, and that at work they can behave badly in the name of 'acting professionally'. For example, loyalty to colleagues requires you to respect confidences. But when that concerns unethical behaviour, you may have a moral responsibility to expose the truth, and become a whistleblower.

People are especially prone to excusing unethical conduct if it involves a good cause. Robbing the rich to feed the poor sounds heroic, but it is still theft and still unethical.

Another excuse is that an action didn't harm anyone. One example is justification of stealing from shops so large they won't notice the effect, or because they are insured. There is never 'no harm'. And the fact that there might be little harm doesn't justify the action, which, again, is still theft.

Another excuse is 'Everyone does it' – and its partner, 'It's always been like that'. That is what used to be said about slavery! These excuses come under what professional ethicists call 'moral conventionalism'.

'I didn't gain anything personally' justifies improper conduct on the false assumption that actions are unethical only where there is a personal advantage.

People who feel they are overworked, underpaid or sometimes both, convince themselves that fringe benefits – such as helping themselves to office stationery, using the work phone or faking a 'sicky' – are fair recompense. Without negotiating these benefits with the employer, it is simply theft.

One example of a rationalisation *par excellence* is the claimed distinction between 'killing' and 'letting die' – where, for example, a terminally-ill patient is left to die from thirst and starvation, rather than being killed outright (see Chapter 23).

*Tu Quoque* (Latin for 'you too') is the assertion that because your accusers are themselves guilty of wrongdoing, they have no right to accuse *you* of doing something wrong. The argument is fallacious because whether your accusers are guilty of wrongdoing is irrelevant to your own responsibility for wrongdoing. Two wrongs don't make a right. One recent example of 'you too' was the claim by US defence secretary Donald Rumsfeld that the public display of American prisoners of war in Iraq breached the Geneva Conventions. In view of America's detainment without trial and ill-treatment of suspects in Camp Delta, Guantánamo Bay, the Iraqi response was that Rumsfeld had no right to point the finger. Rumsfeld may have been guilty of hypocrisy, but the Iraqi counter accusation failed to undermine the validity of his original assertion.

Another excuse for moral prevarication is the *slippery slope argument*. It claims some morally acceptable practice should not be allowed because it will inevitably lead to morally unacceptable consequences. For example, 'sanctioning euthanasia will open the floodgates to the killing of the sick and elderly – look at what happened in Nazi Germany!' This argument is fallacious unless it can be demonstrated that the morally objectionable consequences are indeed inevitable.

## Conclusion

It would seem that most people are happier when they have the approval of their family friends and peers, and that this is often achieved by behaving ethically towards them. But this also applies to Auschwitz Kommandant, Rudolf Höss. He had immense approval from his friends, family, peers, and colleagues. The one glaring criticism is that clearly his idea of relevant stakeholders was not as wide as perhaps it should have been!

On the other hand, how can you explain that some of the greatest and most admired political leaders have behaved so unethically to those outside their immediate circle of stakeholders? One example is Britain's war minister, Winston Churchill's sacrifice of Coventry or his attitude to the fate of millions of east Europeans in his negotiation with Stalin at Yalta.

Perhaps such admiration is explained by the possibility that admirers of such people have themselves failed to appreciate the rights and wishes of relevant stakeholders, or they have drawn the circles of stakeholders too narrowly.

*Dilemma Training* doesn't claim to have all the answers, but it is better than making decisions based on a gut feeling only or merely according to self-interest or expediency. For dilemmas faced by ordinary people with ordinary lives the training can provide an invaluable tool to help work out the sorts of choices they will feel happy with.

And, furthermore, the fact that you have gone through the process of choosing thoughtfully, means that even if your decision turns out to be wrong, in the sense of a bad choice, then it will be easier to live with knowing you did your best to act correctly.

The training also helps relieve the fear of being a fool – of being ripped off – and the resultant tendency to make choices competitively. When you have undertaken the training it is easier to come to terms with the sad fact that in most cases those who act morally will risk being the victim of those who don't. Once you have made it a habit, a principle even, to solve dilemmas ethically, it will matter less that, at a superficial level, you have been disadvantaged, compared with those who act only out of self-interest and expediency.

You can spend years studying philosophy and training in ethical decision making, and be able to talk the ears off anyone who cares to listen. But *walking* the talk is a different matter entirely. Having benefited from the subject's emphasis on dialectic, use and abuse of argument, logic and so on, you might end up with some terrific skills as a lawyer.

But the main point will have been missed if the training leaves you as basically the same old You (except perhaps more argumentative). If, when under extreme pressure, you still act and react in the same old ways, then the training has not achieved its full potential.

It requires a lot of practice before you can make the right decisions under the pressures of daily life. You need to determine the relevant facts and thoroughly understand them, and to be able to predict their likely consequences, as well as to prioritise competing choices. You then need the skills to implement your ethical decisions effectively.

You can't become ethical by simply reading books on the subject. It is a practical matter. Knowledge about ethics is different from *being* ethical. What ethical decision making needs is *direct* experience, to help to make ethical action intuitive, to enable you to *live* it, rather than just to bring it out now and again as a subject for debate. Only then can you claim to have developed your *self*.

This is the role of *Dilemma Training*, which provides you with the means to conduct an honest inner dialogue which will hopefully expose the sort of rationalisations and excuses that can stand in the way of doing the right thing.

Aristotle 384-322 BC

*Dilemma Training* reflects the sort of down-to-earth, practical moral philosophy associated with the ancient Greek philosopher Aristotle and various ancient Chinese philosophies, such as Taoism. It is based on pragmatic wisdom that can underpin a way of life. More than just the application of intelligence, it consists of the ability to make the right ethical decisions in difficult circumstances and under pressure. Such ability is seen as a necessary ingredient for a good life – a flourishing, decent life, for whomever, wherever, whenever.

# 5

## ETHICS – APPLYING THE THEORIES

People make moral judgements daily. On reflection, how do they make those judgements? Do they unreflectively adopt the judgements of their parents, friends, journalists and others around them, or do they think them through for themselves?

In multi-cultural Britain you are faced with the difficulty that what is regarded as right in one (sub-)culture or religion is often regarded as wrong in another. The treatment of women is a good example of this. How do you decide what is the right action in any particular circumstance?

Although there is considerable overlap between values in various societies, the differences demand caution when generalising or appealing to absolute truths. So what makes an action right or wrong? What principles or moral rules can you use on which to base your everyday decisions?

To help you, you need to turn to moral philosophy. It is a vast and complicated area of study, but in order to get to grips with moral issues it is essential to understand the three basic types of moral theory incorporated in it. These three main approaches, which have predominated since the Renaissance, are consequentialism, deontology and virtue ethics. Care-based religious ethics such as the Christian 'golden rule', 'Do unto others as you would have them do unto you', can be seen as coming under deontology.

Virtue ethics theories emphasise the development of virtuous character with which people will themselves flourish as the result of their right actions. Ancient Greek philosopher Aristotle proposed that acquiring virtues is the guide to moral conduct and the achievement of a flourishing life.

Deontological (rule-based) theories hold that actions are intrinsically right or wrong, while consequentialist theories evaluate actions by reference to their consequences. For example, judging whether lying is wrong, a consequentialist will consider the outcome of lying: who benefits? who is harmed? Whereas the deontological approach maintains that lying is wrong under all circumstances *on principle*.

## Do your duty

The most influential deontologist was 19th century German philosopher, Immanuel Kant (1724-1804), who said that moral actions depend solely upon duty without taking any account of the practical consequences they may have. (Deontology derives from the Greek *deon* meaning 'duty' and *logos* meaning 'reason'.)

Applied strictly, the deontological point of view demands that moral decisions should never be made on the basis of their consequences. The moral content of the decision lies in its action, not its predicted outcome. Certain actions are wrong *in themselves* whatever the outcome.

Furthermore, a rational action – premeditated rather than on impulse – is morally correct only if it can be applied universally under all similar circumstances. Kant called this the *Categorical Imperative*.

Universalising our principles makes our actions less liable to be based on self-interest.

Doing your duty makes an action a good action, according to duty-based theories. This would mean, for example, that a woman should look after her terminally-ill mother, not because it will earn her a place in heaven (the possible consequence), but because it is her duty as a daughter to look after her mother.

Religious ethics are examples of duty-based theories. In the Judeo-Christian tradition, for example, various duties are listed in the Ten Commandments. They are absolute, that is, they are true whatever the circumstances or consequences. God is the absolute and external authority to tell us what is right and wrong, good or bad.

This seems straightforward enough, but is not without its problems. God's word is believed to be found in the world's most widely read book, *The Bible*, or in the case of Islam, *The Koran*. The multitude of possible interpretations of these books makes it difficult to determine the right course of action in particular circumstances. Using the same texts, it is possible, for example, to reject all killing but also to justify a 'just war'.

The basic moral principle in the Judeo-Christian tradition is that of the *sanctity of human life*. It originates in *The Bible*, which also states that human beings (but no other beings) are created 'in the image of God'. Humans take up a higher place in the hierarchy of living creatures and can legitimately rule over creatures lower down that same ladder.

All sorts of moral absolutes flow from the sanctity of life principle: the idea that humans have rights, the absolute right to life (even in the womb), and the obligation of trying to keep humans alive regardless of their circumstances.

The Christian 'golden rule' – 'Do unto others as you would have them do unto you' – is similarly rule-based but differs in some important respects. Unlike the *categorical imperative*, it rests on how others should treat you. It is not prescribing a universal law for specific actions – such as telling the truth – but only in general terms the rule that the moral choices you should apply in respect of others should be those you would want to have applied to yourself. On that basis, if you don't mind being lied to, then you are under no obligation yourself to tell the truth.

Many philosophies have been highly influenced by Christian doctrines. Humanists believe that all persons have unique worth and dignity. So did Immanuel Kant, whose ideas were highly influential in the subsequent development of moral philosophy. He expressed the view that human beings should be treated as *ends* in themselves and never as *means*.

For example, being nice to someone because you hope that they would give you a job would be immoral, even if it would enable you to feed your five children who would otherwise starve.

For Kant the motives or intentions behind an action make it a good or bad action, not the consequences. After all, the consequences of our actions are often not within our control, and we can be morally responsible only for what *is* within our control.

The emphasis on *duty* is central to Kantian ethics. An action is a good action when it is based on duty. Importantly, Kant argued that duty is what *reason*, not God, commands. Through reasoning alone we can find guidance about right and wrong actions. All actions have underlying principles or assumptions. Through reasoning we can discover them.

Moral judgements must be made independent of particular circumstances or emotions. This enables a degree of certainty to be achieved in the area of moral conduct. But how does Kant help us decide between potentially conflicting duties such as, for example, our duty to tell the truth and our duty to protect our friends? Sometimes these duties clash. However, in the absence of an external authority to tell us what to do, Kantian ethics – deontology – usefully shows the importance of reason in trying to act morally.

**Think of the consequences**

As the name suggests, consequentialist theories focus on the goodness or badness of the outcomes or consequences of an action. That point of view sanctions the telling of a lie if, for example, it prevents suffering.

Adherents of utilitarianism, a consequentialist (ends-based) doctrine expanded upon by the late 18th, early 19th century English reformers, Jeremy Bentham (1748-1832) and John Stuart Mill (1806-1873), act in a way which aims to promote the greatest happiness to the greatest number of people involved. Where that is not possible they try to do whatever causes the least suffering to the smallest number. The basic doctrine, *act utilitarianism*, is so called because the consequences of the *act* itself are used as a guide for action, and the rightness or wrongness of the act judged accordingly.

A refinement of this, 'rule utilitarianism', considers the hypothetical effect of actions as a general principle – 'What would happen if everyone did it?' The act is 'right' if it is covered by the right rule. The rule is right if the consequences of everyone's actions based on it will promote the greatest happiness or the least suffering. If the act is covered by two conflicting rules, the adherent reverts to act utilitarianism and uses the direct consequences of the act to guide him. Asking the question 'What if everyone did it?' does complicate the case; but the decision is clear.

As a stand-alone system of morality utilitarianism is attractive, but a failure. At best it can serve as a useful guide to moral action, but judging the rightness or wrongness of an action solely by its consequences is only part of the moral process.

Some acts are surely *wrong in themselves* – murder, for example. Others are absolutely rejected by conscience. But utilitarianism cannot cope with this. Bentham gave no room to conscience as a guide to right or wrong. And pleasure? – how do you define it? Utilitarianism assumes domination of pleasure to be synonymous with 'good'; pain and displeasure with 'bad'; but is it? Ask a masochist – or a woman in labour!

And how should pleasure be distributed? One act may produce the greatest amount of happiness, but benefit very few. Another act may produce widely distributed happiness, but less in total quantity. Which do you choose? Utilitarianism offers no guidance.

Nor does it offer guidelines on quantifying happiness. There is the danger that in a society where economic values reign supreme, happiness will be quantified in terms of money or material comfort to the detriment of other values such as love, beauty, natural justice, and so on.

The accuracy of judging consequences is highly questionable, particularly if remote in distance or time. The future is uncertain. An event is like a pebble cast into a pond. How far the ripples go and what that means, we can merely guess. Where do you draw the line between certainty, probability, and guesswork? Utilitarian doctrine doesn't tell you.

Nor does it cope with basic moral questions. Even murder can be justified in some circumstances by applying the *Greatest Happiness Principle*. It doesn't deal with what could be described as 'rock bottom' issues – acts that are good or bad in themselves. Even rule utilitarianism, which does its best to generalise on traditional values such as promise keeping, lying, justice, etc, is on thin ice by virtue of utilitarianism itself. If the utility of breaking a rule in certain circumstances is greater than that of following it, the utilitarian will break it.

Moreover, the greatest happiness principle excludes taking into account the *intrinsic values* a motive for action can have. Surely there is a moral difference between giving money to charity out of disinterested benevolence, and giving it because you are required to do so by your employer?

Utilitarianism cannot stand alone in imposing morals. To bring individual interests more in line with society's interests as a whole, the greatest happiness principle needs to be complemented by criminal law. Whilst theft may create greater happiness for the thief and possibly his family and friends, compared with a little unhappiness for the insured shopkeeper, criminal law will see that he or she is punished, rendered unhappy. The theft will then cause unhappiness all round, and is therefore unjustifiable according to utilitarian ethics.

The fact that an act is good because it generates the most happiness, says nothing about the intention behind it. A bad act can generate good, and vice versa. Charity granted for the sake of knighthood, fame, and further wealth is one example of a bad act with good consequences all round – for the benefactor and the recipient. If a 50 million majority promotes greater happiness by exterminating a six million minority, is that morally justifiable? Again, utilitarianism does not have the answer.

It is a system of morality that is only as good as the person administering it. It was beneficial when applied by benevolent leaders such as the 19th century reformers. They were present as backstop to judge humanely in cases where its strict application would have caused unfair suffering to individuals for the sake of more general pleasure for the many.

If utilitarianism's claim that universal egotism causes everyone to seek their own pleasure, why shouldn't this apply to society's leaders and legislators? Why should they lack self-interest sufficiently to enable them to seek greater happiness of their subjects rather than their own? Utilitarianism demands a strong democracy where legislators are held in check by the people.

Utilitarianism is generally accepted as being elitist – effective only in the hands of a humane ruling class – non-democratic. It could be destructive if applied by the masses, who are hardly ever in a position to judge on matters of widespread greater happiness. Even the utilitarians themselves admitted that the masses need ground rules, like 'thou shalt not kill'.

Despite its glaring inadequacies and inconsistencies as a moral system, utilitarianism was useful in achieving valuable social reform in 19th century Britain. It had the attraction of being a relatively simple theory usually verifiable by empirical facts, and it always provided an answer to a moral problem.

But it has usually been associated with reducing unhappiness rather than direct promotion of positive good. It reduced levels of poverty but was not geared to eliminating it. Spontaneous acts of goodness, such as granting enough income to the poor to raise them out of poverty, were discouraged by the rule utilitarian's questions 'What would happen if we all did it?' 'What would be the consequences?' Utilitarians presumably feared widespread idleness. The kind of conditions Charles Dickens describes in 'A Walk in the Workhouse' (from *Household Words*, Charles Dickens, 1850) reflect the darker side of utilitarianism's application.

### Virtue ethics – Morality without moralising?

*'But we must not follow those who advise us, being men, to think of human things, and being mortal, to think of mortal things, but must, so far as we can, make ourselves immortal, and strain every nerve to live in accordance with the best in us; for even if it be small in bulk, much more does it in power and worth surpass everything.'*

*Aristotle, 'Nicomachean Ethics', X, 7.*

In contrast to the Judeo-Christian tradition, the classical Greek tradition puts more emphasis on *virtue* and *flourishing*. The prime focus is not how we treat *others*, but how we treat *ourselves*. Virtue ethics is primarily concerned with our way of being in the world and with the qualities of character that make us who we are.

Virtue theory's main inspiration is Aristotle (384-322 BC), who wrote that the goal of life is *eudaimonia* (flourishing) – best achieved through the cultivation of various intellectual and moral virtues. Flourishing refers not to the particular mental states you may be experiencing at any particular time, but refers to a longer period of living one's life successfully.

The major philosophical schools that followed Aristotle – the Epicureans, Stoics, and Sceptics – were also concerned with the cultivation of certain virtues, especially those leading to mental tranquillity and freedom from bodily desires. You should bear in mind that the word 'virtue' had a broader meaning for the ancient Greeks than that narrower Christian sense.

For Plato and Aristotle, discovering the virtue of something is simply to discover what it can do best, its function. An axe is virtuous when it cuts wood well. For them it wasn't a moral question, as in what we mean by 'moral' today. However, whereas it might be easy to establish the 'virtue' of an axe in this way, it is considerably more difficult to do so about a complicated organism that has choices.

How can humans choose wisely among their existing options? Aristotle in his *Nicomachean Ethics* concludes that virtues are to be found in the mean between excess and deficiencies, for example, courage is the virtue between the vices of 'too much fear' (cowardice) and 'too little fear' (foolhardiness). Virtues in the virtuous person are harmonised and depend on practical reason. Virtues are not unthinking habits, but require experience, teaching, and reflection so that one makes the right judgements that take into account the specific details of each situation. Which virtues should apply is of course debatable.

Virtue ethics, also known as Neo-Aristotelianism, is concerned more with 'living well' than just the rightness and wrongness of actions. Living well – flourishing – is more than just a sort of passive contentment. It consists of life's struggles and challenges and efforts to overcoming adversity.

In the question, 'how should I live in order to live well?', 'should' has no moral content – unlike the moral prescription, 'you *shouldn't* drink and drive' – but it implies a causal link, as in, 'to reduce the chance of an accident, you shouldn't drink and drive'. This is the major difference between this view of ethics, and the other, more modern western theories, which aim to prescribe moral *should's* as in 'you should be nice to children to be good'.

In most systems of ethics there is a sense that moral behaviour contrasts with self-seeking behaviour. As a result, being ethical is often associated with self-sacrifice. Neo-Aristotelianism fuses the two – to live well (flourish) you should seek excellence of behaviour via the practice of certain virtues. This contains no overt moralising, but simply works out better for the mutual benefit of all concerned, than would, say, either no code of behaviour, or one that demands self-sacrifice. Furthermore, it all comes naturally – according to Neo-Aristotelianism, humans are naturally disposed to flourish through the exercise of 'virtuous' behaviour.

And virtuous behaviour usually has good *consequences*, without the need for utilitarian-type happiness sums. Generosity generates popularity, honesty generates trust, and so on. However, all this is subject to striking the right balance – for example, to be generous, not profligate.

As is the case with other theories, virtue ethics does have its problems:

• the virtuous person can be the victim of the exercise of the virtues, therefore not 'flourish' – for example, honestly owning up to murder, and being gaoled for life. This can be countered with the argument that virtuous behaviour will bring about 'flourishing'; and 'flourishing' is so fundamental to living well, that any other consequences are secondary. On the other hand, Aristotle said, 'Those who maintain that, provided he is good, a man is happy (*eudaemon*) on the rack ... are talking nonsense ...'

- Admittedly, whilst courage is possible on the rack, other virtues, such as generosity, might be a bit impractical. But this just serves to highlight how it seems to be stretching the point to talk about virtues as though they are all directly comparable – generosity, for example, doesn't necessarily carry the same weight of virtuousness as, say, courage. It seems easier to be a generous coward, than a brave meany. And sometimes virtues conflict – for example, not-lying versus loyalty; or saving your own skin out of cowardice, but also out of benevolence for your dependants. What if one's spontaneous honesty led to the death of a loved one?

- Another essential element is achievement of the right balance – not to be stupidly generous, stupidly honest, stupidly courageous. But just how do you know how to get it right?

- Being honest does imply telling the truth effortlessly in circumstances where it would be embarrassing, frightening, or otherwise unpleasant. 'Virtuous' people, who always tell the truth unhesitatingly, seem to do so unthinkingly – otherwise, they might first reflect before deciding whether to tell the truth, and then often be deterred from doing so by negative consequences. Their truthful reaction seems instinctive, somehow determined. There is no evidence that truthfulness can be inherited, so such tendencies are, presumably, culturally determined. But, how do you acquire these virtues, and the habit of applying them unhesitatingly, if you are not brought up to have them? Unless the virtues are fundamentally part of a character, a conscious effort would be required to perform them – and that rules out most forms of spontaneity.

- Whether practising the virtues will help someone to 'live well', depends very much on that person's desires, and the standards of the society in which they have been brought up. There are many wicked people who seem to 'flourish'.

- Neo-Aristotelian ethics has a whiff of elitism about it. For most human beings, morality seems to be tied into survival – physical and social, rather than intellectual. It is possible to argue that honesty, generosity, etc., are basic virtues worth having within a community (village, country, NATO, Mafia, and so on) to ensure its survival. But when deciding how to deal with humans, animals, and things outside those boundaries, virtues at home, for example, honesty, could be vices abroad (especially during conflicts). And, the possibility that today's virtue is tomorrow's vice; or this society's virtue is that society's vice, seems even more likely when virtues stem from issues more remote from the time-honoured basics such as courage and honesty.

- How can you sort out the differences between passive and active application of the virtues – lying and not telling the truth – not being courageous and being cowardly? Take the virtue of honesty. The virtue of truthfulness seems to imply 'love of the truth' – even when truth hurts (yourself and others). And it does not distinguish between 'truth telling' and 'not lying'. The Dutch have an expression that says 'children and drunks tell the truth'. But do they? Or do they simply not lie – either because they do not have the mental wherewithal to construct a lie; or because they simply cannot be bothered; or because they do not have the mental capacity to judge the consequences of telling the truth.

- And, as for 'flourishing', does it all come naturally – are humans naturally disposed to flourish through the exercise of virtuous behaviour? It is not unthinkable that some people might not want to flourish in the generally accepted sense – might not want their projects to be a 'success' – if only to back up their belief in the chaos and meaninglessness of life. Some people thrive on a lack of success – even on illness. Suffering becomes their *raison d'être*; failure their trademark. Unexpected success – say, sudden recovery of good health – would be disastrous for them – especially when their misfortunes have shielded them from life's responsibilities. Neo-Aristotelianism assumes that humans are mainly the kind of creatures that can flourish, and not at each other's expense. In the Neo-Aristotelian world the notion of 'one man's profit is another man's loss' is presumably anathema. A large proportion of 21st century humans, who are quite happy with the way they are 'flourishing' at the expense of others around them under capitalism, would take a lot of convincing of the value of being virtuous in the Neo-Aristotelianism sense.

The concept of personal responsibility coupled with flourishing is reflected in many eastern philosophies. One of them is Taoism. Tao (pronounced 'Dow') is roughly translated as the path, or the way. The Tao is the prime mover of the universe, and maintains balance in the universe through the harmony of opposites (*Yin* and *Yang*). For example, there is no love without hate, no light without dark, no male without female, no up without down. It is a force that flows through all life. Each believer's goal is to become one with the Tao, through inner meditation and contemplation of nature.

The founder of Taoism is reputed to be Lao Tse (604-531 BC), author of the *Tao te Ching*, and a contemporary of political philosopher Confucius. Taoist philosophy has profoundly influenced western culture in areas such as acupuncture, holistic medicine, meditation, and martial arts.

Taoists generally have an interest in promoting health and vitality. They are encouraged to exercise as a means to boost the flow of the body's Ch'i (vital energy). At the same time, the personal development of virtues is paramount, particularly of compassion, moderation, and humility.

Taoists believe that left to their own devices, most people are compassionate by nature. They see in the Tao and in nature the basis of a spiritual approach to living that promotes a stable and unified social order – more stable and enduring than that of governments and other authorities. They emphasise the need to learn, not just *about* nature, but *from* nature.

Communication between East and West was remarkably good even 2,500 years ago. Ancient Taoist ideas filtered through to the West via India to Persia to Greece as long ago as 500BC and were part of the *Zeitgeist* around the time of the major Greek philosophers, such as Aristotle and Plato, 200 years later. Ideas of balance through the harmony of opposites has clearly influenced the Buddhist Golden Middle Way and Aristotle's virtues of balance between excess and deficiency (see above).

The texts of the these Greek philosophers were 'discovered' by western Europeans during the Crusades, but were heavily 'interpreted' to serve the interests of Christendom. To 'rediscover' these ideas in their pre-Christian form, without needing to wrestle with Chinese concepts that were often couched in arcane and obscure metaphorical language, it is worth revisiting the works of the Greeks 500-300BC, and Roman philosophers around the time of Christ.

Particularly in virtue ethics, there is little to distinguish between the virtues of a Taoist monk, a Buddhist Kung Fu warrior, a Persian soldier, a Greek philosopher like Socrates, or, for example, Roman Emperor Marcus Aurelius. And Epicurus has much to offer in terms of a more moderate way of life as an alternative to 21st century McWorld.

**How do you choose your theory?**

It is often assumed that people make the wrong choices – behave badly – because they are more concerned with the consequences – their choices are seen as means to ends. This is associated with the utilitarian approach.

Yet bad behaviour can be equally linked to choices based on a deontological approach, acting on principle or duty, where the principle involved has been inappropriate or too strictly applied. Examples of inappropriate 'duty for duty's sake' have been found in religious fundamentalist crimes and war crimes, and notoriously during the Nazi and Stalinist eras.

Who would you say is the person of integrity – a consequentialist, or a 'duty-for-duty's-sake' Kantian? On the face of it it makes sense to prefer the Kantian. Ethical decisions based on consequences are difficult to predict, because consequences are difficult to predict. With those based on principles, you know what you get. With people of principle you know where you stand.

Acting only according to consequences can encourage self-delusion. 'Acting for the best' could involve kidding yourself that your decision or choice of action will lead to consequences so hard to predict that you could virtually invent them at random. On the other hand, it's much harder to justify breaching a principle than it is to claim after the event that you misjudged the consequences.

On this basis it makes sense to prefer to deal with Rudolf Höss than with Churchill. Yet, this is counter-intuitive. We know instinctively that this cannot possibly be right.

After consulting the very different ethical theories, when considering moral dilemmas, how do you decide which to apply? Unfortunately there is no neat answer, partly because the question reflects only part of the problem. At best you need to apply all of them.

Perhaps it could be argued that ethics cannot change people's fundamental prejudices about what is right and wrong. But philosophical reflection can at least help to bring those assumptions to the surface where one can examine them either as an individual or, ideally, in groups. Ethical thought is a creative process. No one set of rules can assure outcomes that in the long run will be found to have been the 'right' ones. But it is quite clear that ethical discussion does produce better quality decisions.

And what about an intuitive sense of right and wrong? Despite all the moral calculations done in your head, you are still likely to be left with a gut feeling about the right thing to do. Dilemma Training doesn't ignore this. It takes account of those important intuitive feelings when arriving at a decision.

**Finally, you need to make sure that the resultant decision has been carefully thought through, does not appeal to external authorities, and can be applied in similar circumstances – that it is 'universalisable' – and that you can realistically act upon it.**

# 6

# USE AND ABUSE OF ARGUMENT

---

*'We think we know more because we have increased the number of symbolic expressions and learned phrases. We hardly pay any attention to the fact that all these skills are only the scaffolding of science, and not science itself.'*

*Georges-Louis Leclerc, Comte de Buffon (1707-1788), 'How to Study Natural History'.*

---

'Obscurantism' is a formidable-looking word describing the use of strange, formidable language to hide knowledge from others. Obscurantism is a hallmark of most trades and professions. They are shrouded in mysticism and unintelligible jargon because either their practitioners want to protect their knowledge, or their disciples want to hide the fact that they have not understood it.

Take medicine for example. You think you have cracked your shin playing football. By the time you reach hospital you have got a suspected fracture of the tibia. You are horrified to hear you have apparently got a lesion to the patella; but mightily relieved when this turns out simply to be a bruised knee.

The medical profession, there to save lives and to heal, protects its authority and importance with walls of technical jargon couched mainly in Latin. Those dedicated to preservation of life are dedicated to a dead language.

Foreign and jargon words are essential where they replace laborious description, but only where they are clearly understood by all concerned – not where they serve merely to throw a smokescreen over understanding.

To make a good ethical decision requires making an informed decision, and that demands cutting through esoteric concepts and arcane language. This is not to deny the efficacy of metaphor in aiding understanding, but to criticise its role in obscurantism couched in oblique metaphor for the sake of preserving it from non-initiates.

Ethical decisions are underpinned by argument – implicit and explicit – by giving reasons to justify an action or judgement. Even someone whose ethical development is so advanced that they intuitively do the right thing – if such people exist – may need to argue their case after the event.

When deciding on the right courses of action there are plenty of traps awaiting the unwary. The most dangerous of these is the abuse of argument, where sophistic devices can be used to justify rationalisation and excuses. This is a particular danger when working in a group to solve a dilemma, or even when trying to reach a decision alone, when such tricks of argument enter your own personal rhetoric, and rationalisation and wishful thinking impair your judgement.

**What is an argument?**

An argument consists of one or more *premises*, and a conclusion. The premises contain the reasons supporting the conclusion. The conclusion is the statement expressing the belief supported by the argument.

The classic argument quoted by traditional books about logic derives from Aristotle. It runs as follows:

Premise 1.     All men are mortal.
Premise 2.     Socrates was a man.
Conclusion:   Therefore, Socrates was mortal.

This is known as a syllogism.

An argument can be valid, or true, or both valid and true.

A valid argument is one where the conclusion logically follows from the premises.

| | |
|---|---|
| Premise 1. | All men are immortal. |
| Premise 2. | Socrates was a man. |
| Conclusion: | Therefore, Socrates was immortal. |

This is a valid argument. But it is not true.

An argument can be true, but not valid.

| | |
|---|---|
| Premise 1. | All men are mortal |
| Premise 2. | Socrates was mortal. |
| Conclusion: | Therefore, Socrates was a man. |

This is an invalid argument. Its conclusion is a *formal fallacy* – or, for Latin lovers – *non sequitur*, meaning 'it doesn't follow'.

The above arguments are *deductive*. This means that if their premises are true, then their conclusion must be true.

**The inductive argument**

Another type of argument – but less conclusive – is known as an inductive argument.

The classic example is:
The sun has always risen in the East.
Therefore, the sun will rise in the East tomorrow.

This argument is *deductively* invalid, but is a strong *inductive* argument. Its conclusion is most probably true given the truth of the premise. Inductive arguments are not just either true or false, as in the case of deduction. They vary from very weak to very strong.

## Arguments underpinning ethical decision making

An example of deductive *moral* argument is:

Any action that involves dishonesty is wrong.
This action involves dishonesty.
Therefore, this action is wrong.

Valid *moral* arguments must include a statement of a general moral value – for example, 'Any action that involves *dishonesty* is wrong' and a statement of relevant facts – for example, 'This action involves dishonesty'.

Although this structure seems quite simple, moral reasoning often involves not one but several moral values, and a whole series of arguments leading to the final conclusion. Sorting out these arguments is the role of *Dilemma Training*.

Also, such a conclusion from such an argument must be able to be consistently applied in different situations. It must be *universalisable*. If, for example, you conclude that it is wrong to torture Americans because torture is inherently wrong, then you are committed to concluding that it would be equally wrong to torture non-Americans for the same reason.

The *formal fallacy* mentioned above is just one among many fallacies that obscure valid and true arguments.

There are numerous examples of false argument and tricks of sophistry. The more common ones include:

*The Naturalistic Fallacy*
When someone simply describes 'natural' facts as the basis for moral judgement, without citing any principles, they commit a 'natural fallacy'. Take, for example, an argument for slavery:

Slavery has been carried on for thousands of years in all sorts of cultures.

Therefore, there is nothing wrong with slavery.

The argument fails because the main premise doesn't state a moral value. A better argument might be:

Employment brings out the best in people.
Slavery provides employment.
Therefore slavery brings out the best in people.

But, although an improvement, this is open to challenge on the definition of 'employment', which is usually held to mean 'gainful' employment.

*Argument to the People*
An argument to the people in support of a particular moral judgement appeals to popular prejudices shared by members of a group. Usually without any logical justification for its assertions, it aims to inflame the passions of that group to get them to accept a certain moral conclusion. Mass immigration's threat to British people's jobs and housing has been a classic example of such argument, including Enoch Powell's 'Rivers of Blood' speech in 1968.

*Crafty Conflation*
This involves running a number of ideas together, which may seem similar, but where they have very different meanings. For example, an association of chemical producers tried to defend the use of chemicals in food and the environment on the basis that the environment is already made up of chemicals – that everything is made up of chemicals, even water itself. This was an example of crafty conflation between the term 'chemical' and what environmentalists were objecting to which were toxic chemicals.

*Emotive Language*
Emotive language occurs when value-laden words are used where other more neutral terms could be just as useful. The words 'terrorist' and 'freedom-fighter' are examples of emotive words, which, when used in arguments, need to

be countered with more neutral, fact-words. Emotive words might be useful to stir up action, but they are a distraction and have no place at the ethical decision-making stage.

*Rash Generalisation (All Xs are Y)*
This often takes the form of Xs are Y – e.g., women are bad drivers; Dobermans are vicious. It takes only one example of an X that isn't Y to disprove this assertion.

*The Persuaders*
Conscious use of persuaders can be another way of trying to trick others into accepting an unsupported assertion, such as:
'It is obvious that...'
'Only a fool would fail to realise that...'
'Anyone with any intelligence would agree that...'
'The facts speak for themselves...'
'If you're honest with yourself...'

*Begging the Question*
This means to offer an argument in which the conclusion to be argued for is already stated in the premises.
For example: All Belgians are boring;
Counterargument: I know Belgians that are not boring.
Response: Then they can't be real Belgians.

An example of a question-begging question would be 'When did the universe begin?' which already assumes unquestioningly that the universe *did* begin. A more honest version would be 'Did the universe have a beginning? If it did, when did it begin?' or 'If we can assume that the universe had a beginning, when was it?'

*The Red Herring*
This is the diversion to another question, to a side issue, or by irrelevant objection. For example, 'Not enough is being done to combat global warming';
Counter: 'France alone spent millions to help the elderly cope with hot summers'.

*The argument that we should not combat X, which is admittedly evil, because there is a worse evil Y* against which our efforts should be directed – for example, the assertion that we should not combat child poverty at home because we need to fight the war on terrorism.

*Emphasising the logical correctness* of an argument, where the premises contain doubtful or untrue statements of fact:
Every man has his price;
You are a man;
Therefore, you have your price.

*Argument in a circle:*
All prisoners in Camp Delta are terrorists.
How do you know they're terrorists?
If they weren't terrorists they wouldn't be there.

*Changing the meaning of a term* during the course of an argument. Children need schools that offer a caring environment;
This government is committed to improving the environment.

*The use of a false dichotomy,* which ignores the continuous series of possibilities between the two extremes presented.
If you're not a socialist, you must be a fascist;
or, if you're not with us you must be against us.

*Suggestion by repeated affirmation* – confidently repeating your assertion over and over again, without appearing to consider any counterarguments.

*Suggestion by using a confident manner.*

*Suggestion by prestige* – 'as the president of this great nation...'

*Prestige by using pseudo-technical jargon* (obscurantism).

*The appeal to authority* – 'to resolve the question just consult the Ten Commandments'.

*Finding ways to needle an opponent* to make him argue badly.

## Necessary and sufficient conditions

A way of determining the definition of something, for example, 'integrity' – is by using 'necessary and sufficient conditions' – a useful tool employed by professional ethicists and philosophers in general. In this case, suppose a choice of action is proposed as a definitive condition of integrity – say being truthful. You can test it in two ways. First, you can ask whether there is any example of integrity that does not include truthfulness. If you cannot find such an example, truthfulness must be a *necessary* condition of integrity. Secondly, you can ask whether some things have truthfulness, but do not involve integrity. For example, someone may be consistently truthful, but lack other components of what is usually meant by 'integrity'. Then truthfulness, whilst a necessary condition of integrity, is not a *sufficient* condition of it.

To summarise: if integrity is defined by truthfulness, then anyone that is considered to have integrity must have the quality of truthfulness (a necessary condition), but anyone that has truthfulness need not have integrity (it is not a sufficient condition).

## Essential reading

There is a large number of books on the use and abuse of argument. One of the most comprehensive and humorous is *Straight and Crooked Thinking* by Robert H. Thouless. It deals with 38 dishonest arguments, many of which are described above.

There isn't sufficient space here to deal with the entire armoury of various 'devices' in detail, nor to cover an exhaustive list of examples of poor reasoning. Apart from Robert Thouless' book, two others are essential to an understanding of the guises and pitfalls of bad argument. One is *Thinking from A to Z* by Nigel Warburton, and the other is *Critical Thinking for AS Level* by educational consultant Roy van den Brink-Budgen.

# 7

# CRY FREEDOM!

"ARE BIRDS EVER FREE FROM THE CHAINS OF THE SKYWAY?"
— BOB DYLAN

To effectively make an ethical decision, you have to be free to do so – free to express your values and your feelings. It could be argued that Sophie's choice was not a choice at all. A real choice is supposed to depend on its being made by someone who has complete freedom of choice. But what does it mean to be 'free'?

'Freedom' is commonly regarded as something intrinsically good and desirable. But what exactly is it? Shouting from the hill top 'I am free' could mean a wide variety of things: your divorce has come through; a therapist has cured you of your hang-ups; you've been released on bail.

Philosophers do agree about one aspect of freedom – it is *an absence of constraint*, sometimes known as *negative freedom*. This usually refers to constraints imposed from 'outside' – external constraints such as preventing girls from attending school (as is the case in some countries); preventing women from giving birth at home because it is against a surgery's policy; or forcing people to wear a seat belt, because it is the law. Within this framework, being constrained from driving a car because you don't know how, or because you are disabled, is not seen as being denied freedom.

It is not easy to pinpoint the relevant *natural* – as opposed to *human* – factors which establish whether or not someone is free. For example, each day people die of poverty and hunger. Yet there is enough food in the world for everyone. The problem is political and economic – a lack of distribution of available resources. Those responsible – and how do you pinpoint responsibility? – for maintaining this *status quo* could be said to be 'constraining' the victims of poverty, denying them freedom, or even removing it altogether through death.

There is a huge difference between various kinds of constraints on freedom. For example, a lack of freedom as a result of advertising – 'automatically' buying a particular brand of cereal, because the name sounds familiar – differs markedly from the lack of freedom you experience when a mugger forces you to hand over your wallet. One way to fix a point on this continuum – less free to more free – is to look at the consequences of removing the constraint. In the case of mugging, the consequence of your defying the constraint the mugger imposes on you could be your death. Of course, psychological consequences such as intimidation and hurt pride are more difficult to assess.

Man is born free but is forever in chains.
Jean-Jacques Rousseau 1712-1778.

How could we apply the above criteria to restriction of animals' freedom? Is it worse to deny a bird the freedom to fly or a nocturnal animal the freedom to roam at night, than to constrain other aspects of an animal's behaviour that are less 'typical' of its particular species? In other words, the criteria assume not only that we can indeed compare different consequences and their comparative value, but they also necessitate asking the living creature concerned. This cannot be done with, for example, babies, animals or someone in a coma.

If an individual or an entire group of people has been influenced to such an extent by a religious leader or political ideology, that they actually *want* what their leader wants, are they really free? They *probably feel* free. They would probably say they can do what they want, and are therefore free from constraints. The problem is that freedom in this scenario depends on what the individual feels or experiences. It seems to be a subjective matter. In contrast, we do believe that it *is* possible to distinguish between people's conscious adoption of other people's thinking and ideas, as against their 'mindless' absorption of others' ideas.

Sometimes the price for acting differently is relatively small. But there is another necessary condition for genuine choice — that someone understands the possible alternatives. Sometimes more information is necessary; at other times the opportunity to think through other possible alternatives is all that is needed. Also, you can have many possibilities of choice at one level of importance, but have choice restricted at more important levels. For example, Britain has many political parties to choose from, but freedom of choice is still limited to the wider democratic political framework.

Such considerations lead to a more 'positive' definition of freedom – freedom as the absence of social and cultural forces, enabling self-realisation, creative initiatives and autonomy. As opposed to freedom *from* external constraints, this is a freedom *to*, for example, flourish as a person.

A *liberal* solution would be to argue that the freedom of individuals should be restricted only when not to do so would cause harm to others – when others would have less freedom. As a criterion this is helpful only if we clarify the meaning of 'cause harm'. Liberals often make it a priority that the freedom of one individual should not be at the expense of someone else's freedom. Laws to protect individuals' freedom serve to protect liberties such as freedom of expression, religion, travelling or voting.

English philosopher John Stuart Mill (1806-1873) devoted his entire book *On Liberty* to defending the idea that the only reason a society should prevent someone from doing something is that it harms someone else. In his view, the only justification for interfering with someone else's freedom is self-protection. Individuals have the right to express their beliefs freely, even when they contradict widely held political, religious or moral beliefs. However, there is a problem here with what is meant by 'harm'. Expressing atheist beliefs, or satirizing religious dogma, for example, could deeply offend some people. Is this a good reason to temper one's speech?

It may be the case that in Europe we are all free to get an education, or to choose where we live. But it could be argued that unless governments encourage early educational opportunities, and help with adequate nutrition and support, children from poorer families are less free than those from more well-off families, in the sense that they are less able to exploit opportunities for self-realisation.

**Is individual freedom possible if we are not all equal? Philosopher Karl Marx (1818-1883) and his followers believed that positive freedom is impossible without economic and social equality. Class divisions cause alienation and prevent you from expressing your real essence. Equality precedes freedom.**

# 8

## I AM FIT, THEREFORE I THINK

FROM STRENGTH CAME FORTH SWEETNESS

Good decision making depends on good quality thinking. And that depends on having a clear head. The efficacy of the ethical decision-making process is considerably impaired if you are tired, run down and/or generally unfit. Physical fitness is essential to mental fitness. There are endless ways of achieving physical fitness in the West, but before you take your pick it is worth taking a look at some eastern alternatives.

The interesting point about eastern philosophies is that they rarely make the distinction between the mental and the physical. Fitness of an integrated mind and body is a condition of integrity. A Kung Fu warrior would have been expected to embody the paradigm of virtue and integrity.

Even more interesting from the point of view of *Dilemma Training* is that the concept of personal responsibility is very strongly reflected in eastern philosophies and the martial arts associated with them. One example is Tai Ch'i Chuan; another is Kung Fu, deriving respectively from the ancient philosophies of Taoism and Buddhism. The ethics of both are reflected in those of the ancient Greeks, and Aristotle in particular. The good person is the person who, through training, knows intuitively the right way to act, who is fit for right action.

Personal responsibility is paramount. Respect, but do not blindly follow, your teacher or any other 'authority', or you run the risk of losing your unattached personality and ideas – of losing your *self*. Practitioners of, for example, Yi Quan Kung Fu, claim that books and teachers are to be consulted only. You have to advance by yourself. If you fail, you have no right to blame your teacher. If you think he was a bad teacher, then you've only got yourself to blame for choosing him.

The exercises associated with the martial arts aim primarily at increasing a person's store of energy (known as *Ch'i*) and structuring the body to enable *ch'i* to flow efficiently. This is done through exercises aimed at stretching tendons and ligaments, improving posture, increasing strength, exercising the heart, and eating a balanced (*yin/yang*) diet.

At the advanced stage of Yi Quan, for example, your intuition is awakened, you are able to detect imminent problems or dangers, and to respond appropriately. Prepared actions are left behind. In this state of consciousness, the basis of action is your liberated intuition. This intuition is helpful in your work and at home, providing an enhanced sense of self-confidence, and a greater awareness of life's opportunities and threats.

A study of Taoism and/or Buddhism (especially Zen) is regarded as essential to an understanding of southeast Asian martial arts. One problem is to sort out authentic Taoist texts from the New Age material that is around. On the other hand, Buddhism is far more firmly established and its texts more authentically presented through Buddhist societies worldwide. And many Taoist ideas are present in Buddhism, but couched in different terms (and language).

**Whatever path you choose towards physical well-being, the results will be the sort of mental alertness essential to effective choices of action.**

'Strength'

# PART II

# 9

# DILEMMA TRAINING IN ACTION

---

*'Dilemma training is a useful instrument to foster moral competence and a culture of moral awareness in profit and non-profit organisations. It triggers the attention, makes people more self-confident, and it opens the way to a culture of discussion instead of commands. At the end of the day, the long way of fostering integrity may well prove to be the most effective one.'*

*Professor Henk van Luijk, director, European Institute for Business Ethics, Nyenrode University in the Netherlands.*

---

*Dilemma Training* helps people not only as individuals but also as members of organisations to examine and discuss ethical choices, and seek solutions to them. It is *empowering*. By encouraging you to think for yourself, it gives you the feeling of *being in charge* of your actions and your life.

During group sessions the facilitator helps participants to focus on their real-life ethical dilemmas, or on those chosen from current affairs or a work of fiction. They then draw out the values, assumptions and intuitive reasoning underpinning their initial responses.

Participants then examine questions such as *Who has interests and rights? Have we got enough information? Is it really my decision? What are the pros and cons? Am I prepared to ignore arguments that do not serve my cause? How do I weigh up the arguments?*

Ethical behaviour can involve two basic types of choice. One is a *moral decision* – a choice between doing the right thing as against a wrong action. Examples include whether or not to break the law, lie intentionally or break the code of values of a community. Not all such decisions stem from dilemmas. 'I have decided to use the work phone for private use 'cos I hate the boss' does not spring from a dilemma.

The other type of choice, dealt with by the training, is the *ethical dilemma* – a choice between two or more right actions. Examples include choice between telling the truth vs loyalty; values across different cultures; raising social standards vs commitments to profitability for shareholders; individual vs community interests; moral behaviour at work vs behaviour at home; short-term vs long-term interests; environmental performance vs profitability and continued employment; justice vs compassion. It is this type of choice that is usually meant when referring to 'ethical decision making'.

The training illustrates how ethical dilemmas arise in everyday life in relationships with those around us. Examples include a duty of loyalty to a family member versus a duty to disclose that the person has committed a crime; or a duty to drive an injured neighbour as quickly as possible to hospital versus a duty to observe the highway code.

Participants are introduced to a *six-step thinking tool* that they can use themselves in their personal and professional lives. Even if the decisions taken using this tool fail to turn out to be the right ones in terms of the consequences, participants at least have the satisfaction of knowing that they *themselves* justified their decision *ethically*.

During the basic training, participants gain insight into the meaning of 'integrity', and the social context of a dilemma, as well as acquaintance with questioning the ethical aspects of their actions.

The method was originally developed by the European Institute for Business Ethics at the University of Nyenrode in the Netherlands and was adapted for application in government by Governance & Integrity of Amsterdam, and in Britain and Eire by ethics consultants, Dialogue Works. It has been successfully employed by local government, the armed forces, inland revenue, the police and in education.

The training programme creates people who are morally competent when faced with complex situations. They can make effective moral judgements for themselves and for the organisations they work for. The training helps workers to address ethical choices effectively, to discuss them efficiently and to find and agree on methods of integrating them within the organisation's mainstream objectives in situations where correct ethical behaviour is not immediately clear.

During sessions the facilitator helps the participants to focus on their real-life ethical dilemmas encountered in the workplace. The values and assumptions underlying possible responses are uncovered and carefully examined by the group. The model enables critical and creative thinking with others about the often implicit and intuitive reasoning that guides our actions. This opens up new avenues of decision making.

It is crucial for an organisation such as, for example, a government department, that management and staff are conscious of the fact that their work contributes to establishing or maintaining justice among the country's people. That is why management and staff should be asking not only 'how effective are my actions?', but also *are my actions ethical?* They also need to be able to *answer* these questions.

The method is an instrument *par excellence* to stimulate, support and reward the independent ethical decision making of every civil servant. It gives an enormous impulse to reflection and discussion about ethical questions within the organisation. It enables management and staff to take part in a community of ethical enquiry within and beyond their own departments.

Management and staff can stand up to scrutiny. They can explain their actions, and morally justify them. Because they feel they have nothing to fear and nothing to hide, they work in a more relaxed and efficient manner, get on better with each other, have greater job satisfaction, and take less sick leave. The entire organisation becomes more democratic.

The training strengthens individuals' ethical decision making under operational circumstances and enables each participant to recognise right courses of action. Participants are introduced to the six-step thinking tool that they can use themselves in their personal and professional lives. At the same time, the training enables participants to use this inclusive method as an effective intervention to tackle most issues central to the running of a good organisation.

The programme has been developed to help make careful and balanced decisions when confronted with dilemmas. It offers a conceptual framework, which allows people on an individual basis or in consultation with others, to arrive at an informed decision when confronted with moral dilemmas or situations where it is difficult to decide. Importantly, the model enables a person to account for a particular decision taken after the event, both personally, and to others.

The method can be used as the first step to develop an organisation's ethical code and to shape a more ethical organisation.

It is recommended for all levels of management, not least because it explores the concept of moral leadership, so essential to meeting pressures on contemporary issues such as corporate social responsibility and sustainable development.

The bedrock of good Corporate Social Responsibility, in addition to the duty towards shareholders, involves responsible conduct towards employees, contractors, suppliers, customers, society (e.g., Inland Revenue), and the environment. The corporation needs not only to behave ethically, but also to develop sensitivity to the needs and opinions of society at large.

In a post-Enron era, there is a growing global concern about a perceived decline in ethical behaviour, and especially a decline in public and corporate morality.

In business, 'good' behaviour needs to rest on management having a deep core of ethical values that gives them the courage and skills to make difficult choices, and resolve painful dilemmas.

*Dilemma Training* helps managers discuss, agree with stakeholders, and formulate an effective code of practice – defensive (reactive – avoiding litigation, complying with legislation, etc.) and offensive (proactive – such as anticipating new regulation, and improving public image).

Examples of core moral values in business include: exercise your duty to shareholders, don't lie, don't cheat, don't steal, don't bribe, care for stakeholders (employees, community, environment, etc).

The training is used mainly to help apply the corporations' code of ethics when faced with difficult ethical dilemmas – resolving conflicting choices of 'right' action, taking real-life examples from participants and showing how they impact on the company and staff.

The chapters in Part II examine how the training is applied in certain areas of activity such as education, combating substance abuse, local government, business, the military and the media.

# 10

## EDUCATION

## LESSONS FROM A MAN CHILD

*May you grow up to be righteous, May you grow up to be true.*
*May you always know the truth, And see the lights surrounding you.*
*May you always be courageous, Stand upright and be strong.*
*May you stay forever young.*

I WAS SO MUCH OLDER THEN,
I'M YOUNGER THAN THAT NOW.

There's a little lad living on the west coast of Wales who is so virtuous he'd be too good for the priesthood. He is keen to share, he empathises with others' suffering, he is sensitive to the moods of others, he is spontaneous, and he has a great sense of humour. All these are ends in themselves. None of these virtues is coloured by the vices of self-consciousness or their use as means to ends. He is free from the 'curse of purposes' – so far.

He can clearly conceptualise and categorise – all food is 'Marmite', all cats are 'Sasha', all brothers are 'Tim'.

He is only two and a half. His name is Liam.

Observing and listening to Liam confirms the conviction that 'child' and 'adult' are arbitrary and misleading categories. A person is not *either* a child *or* an adult.

A person simply *changes* over time, gaining some aspects on the way through life, and losing others – for example, losing innocence, gaining scepticism, regaining innocence and losing scepticism; gaining practical skills and then eventually losing them; losing spontaneity, gaining self-consciousness, losing self-consciousness; regaining spontaneity; losing fearlessness, gaining fear of rejection, ridicule, failure, poverty, violence, pain, death, and then finally losing those fears.

A person's life can be seen as a circular continuum, along which many changes can be plotted, and on which many aspects encountered at the beginning reappear at the end. A flourishing life depends partly on the need to surrender to those changes, rather than resisting them in the struggle to be 'adult' and avoid being a 'child'.

Developing a virtuous disposition has little to do with metamorphosing from one state of being – child, to another state of being – adult. It has to do with development in an environment of interaction with others, care for others, and – 'education, education, education!'

## A-moral, im-moral or differently moral?

Young people's behaviour has always troubled parents and teachers. Public concern – fed by media hype – is fuelled by a perceived decline in values and in respect for authority, leaving a so-called moral vacuum. Breakdown of families, increased crime, bad language, disobedience at school, binge drinking and drugs misuse – fed by media hype – paint a picture of a society that has lost it way. People can apparently no longer tell right from wrong. There is little agreement about who is at fault. Teachers blame parents, parents point the finger at schools, others blame the government, poverty, unemployment and even the absence of military service.

But is there really a moral vacuum? Are young people really more a-moral or im-moral than previous generations? There are signs to the contrary – that there is, in fact, more concern for the rights of others. There is definitely a greater tolerance towards the elderly, gays, women, different races, foreigners, animals, children and the environment. Corporal punishment in schools, perfectly acceptable in Britain until fairly recently, has been abandoned. Many habits of thought and behaviour are increasingly examined on moral grounds. Educational institutions talk about participation, tolerance, diversity and children's rights. Universities have ethics committees and now take research ethics seriously.

It is not clear, however, to what extent such political changes are an accurate reflection of what most people do indeed genuinely *think* and *feel* – or to what extent they reflect blind obedience to political correctness (being PC). This has spread from academia into government and now dominates school policy and teaching practice. In other words, are people acting more ethically because they feel it's right to do so, or because they are afraid of not being PC? There's still an abundance of sexist and racist jokes. What has changed is they are told when there are no women or black people around to object.

Despite its intention to redistribute power from the powerful to the powerless, political correctness has become a tyrannical ideology, defining what can and cannot be discussed in public, and even in private. It shapes what people regard as controversial, and encourages censorship in education. It also undermines people's confidence to express what they really believe. It discourages young people from exploring the world as it really is, populated by real people, good bad and indifferent – a school for sinners – rather than an imaginary world of PC saints.

Teachers often 'protect' their pupils by avoiding controversial issues where there might be a risk of politically *incorrect* answers or outcomes. Children might get upset; parental protest is best avoided.

Perhaps teachers care too much. They might be a little out of touch with what children really experience and the kind of influences they are exposed to outside school. The urge to protect can stifle independence of thought.

The legally binding United Nations (UN) *Convention on the Rights of the Child* spells out children's rights. They have a right to 'freedom of thought', to 'express opinions' and to 'have a say in matters affecting their own lives'. Yet, in practice, the content and the procedure of classroom discussion is decided by adults on children's behalf.

Schools are usually hierarchical and undemocratic – not the most suitable environment in which to experience real democratic decision-making. What young people think makes little difference to what they are taught, how they are taught and who teaches them. This powerlessness to effect any significant change, coupled with a lack of equality and respectful treatment, can trigger deep resentment, anger, disaffection and boredom – not only in young people, but even in some teachers.

Anti-social behaviour can often be directly linked to the

experience of school. These are often dealt with in education by 'anger management' strategies. But these are just yet more instruments to control behaviour and avoid facing up to the basic political injustice of the educational system.

## Living up to the convention

Most educational institutions are not living up to the terms of the UN convention. This is the result of some deeply engrained assumptions about childhood. Children are still regarded as not being reasonable or 'mature'. They are usually viewed as egocentric and unable to distinguish between right and wrong. If they do behave well, it is assumed they do so only out of fear of punishment.

Romantic notions about children and their innocence still prevail. At the same time, adults believe the opposite – that children are uncultivated, wild and in need of taming. Both positions fail to regard them as responsible, reasonable partners in discussion about important issues. Teaching 'Reasoning' – the fourth 'R' – is perhaps even more appropriate to a rapidly changing world than the other three 'Rs', reading, 'riting and 'rithmetic.

Children are citizens, not just citizens-to-be, and they should have the freedom to help shape the rules they themselves will be subjected to. Claims that young children are not 'mature' enough for such responsibility rest either on psychological assumptions about the 'stages' of their development – based on the theories of psychologists such as Piaget and Kohlberg – or on outworn philosophical assumptions about what is meant by 'rationality'.

Nonetheless, a lot has happened within academic philosophy in the last two decades to justify the claim that young children can do 'real' philosophy, including ethics. Also, several psychologists have challenged the idea that children cannot de-centre in the imagination. This opens the way to accepting that they are able to empathise in their reasoning

– essential for ethical decision-making. This view is reflected in the works of anthropologist Margaret Donaldson and the philosopher of education Gareth Matthews.

## Autonomy and equality

To regard young people as being at the epicentre of the current so-called moral crisis misses the point. It is the march of democratisation that lies at the root of the moral 'crisis'. This is because it brings with it the core values of *autonomy* and *equality*. And these demand a vigorous, critical attitude towards authoritarian moral guidance.

Young people no longer unquestioningly accept what they are told to do or think. In the West, people rarely see themselves as part of a larger order dictating their 'station in life'. They now assume their right to choose their own way of life and have much more freedom to decide which values to live by.

Individuals want to shape their own lives on the basis of what they value and find important. Although this ideal of self-fulfilment has been criticised as selfish and egocentric, the underlying moral principle of *authenticity*, of being true to oneself, is a strong moral force that needs to be taken seriously if moral education is to be effective and meaningful. This is closely linked to *autonomy* – having the freedom to decide for yourself what and who you want to be.

But this can conflict with the needs of others. Having such choices can be a heavy burden. How do you choose for the best?

Education's greatest challenge is to teach ways in which individuals learn to make decisions that go beyond the self – that provide the discipline to construct arguments to include all stakeholders in decision making. This is one of the core features of *Dilemma Training*.

## What schools are doing

Schools play a central role in shaping young people's thinking, their self-image and their attitudes to others. Social values are taught implicitly or explicitly. *Explicit* moral guidance is given, for example, in Citizenship, Religious Education and Personal, Social, Health Education (PSHE) and also through codes of conduct and punishments. However, codes of conduct are usually drawn up by the school management without pupils' involvement.

How do we know what pupils really feel about the difficult decisions they make daily at school? What obstacles stand in the way of doing what teachers believe is morally right? Lists of rules for good conduct remind pupils they should, for example, respect others, be honest and polite, fair and tolerant. These express important values and can contribute to making a school a more pleasant, safer learning environment. However, if they do not reflect the wishes, rights or interests of all stakeholders, such as parents, governors, pupils, teachers and support staff, they will not be effective.

Also, abstract recommendations such as 'be honest' or 'be fair' wrongly suggest that figuring out what it means to be fair or honest is straightforward. To make use of such abstract virtues in concrete situations, you need to be taught how to make good judgements.

Values are not only taught explicitly in schools, but also *implicitly* in a variety of ways. These include the ways teachers interact with pupils, their choices of teaching methods and the teaching curriculum. If those values are made explicit, they can be examined for their moral themes and conflicts.

## Feelings or reason?

The rejection of authority accompanying democratisation, has led to the other extreme, *relativism*. This is the idea that 'anything goes', that everyone has the right to their own beliefs and opinions. Even education acquiesces to this assumption through its curriculum content and prescribed pedagogies. 'Circle time', for example, presents an opportunity to explore other people's beliefs and opinions. But it does not encourage children to challenge those beliefs on moral grounds. 'Who am I to question your beliefs…?' is a common response.

Another major obstacle to ethical decision-making is *moral subjectivism* – the idea that moral positions are not grounded in reason, but that we adopt them, because they feel right, or because we feel drawn to them. Reasons need to be independent of choice and justified on their own merit. A Learning Support Assistant's wearing a Muslim veil cannot be justified merely by pointing out that it is her choice. She needs to give a reason. Otherwise it would become as morally insignificant as choosing between blue or black jeans.

Another difficulty is *instrumental rationality*. This calculates the most economical means to achieve certain ends. Success is measured in terms of efficacy. Pupils, but also teachers, are often treated as instruments or raw materials to achieve certain objectives. This can be the success of the school measured through league-tables or the success of the pupil to achieve good exam results. Treatment of individuals as ends in themselves, as people with dignity in their own right, can be sacrificed to achieve a particular outcome.

When choosing between two courses of actions, the question 'what is the morally right thing to do?' is often subservient to the question 'what is the most efficient thing to do?'. It assumes that it is possible to address the question without addressing the moral dimension of the decision. However, the moral point of view is not one among a competing set of options. It has already asserted itself, and needs to be dealt with.

In education moral decisions are made all the time. When a head teacher is trying to balance the interests of governors, parents, pupils, and other members of the community she has a moral problem, because she has to decide the priority of these interests in the total scheme of the organisation. To celebrate Christmas, for example, in a majority Muslim school would be an example of such an ethical decision. The final decision would need to take account of the rights and wishes of all relevant stakeholders.

Teachers are keen to be seen to be tolerant. But tolerance doesn't mean an uncritical acceptance of what others say or do. Just because something is valuable to someone doesn't make it a value. The fact that it is someone's *choice* to do something – to wear a veil in school, to censor a book, to expel a pupil – doesn't make it worthwhile *per se*. The fact that it is someone's choice doesn't make it a worthwhile *reason*.

Tolerance is the acceptance that others may be different, but also that their viewpoints are worth investigating in a reasoned dialogical manner. The outcome may be that certain positions are rejected as morally wrong. It is possible to be tolerant of someone and still disagree with them.

The challenge is to teach moral reasoning and to raise awareness of the intrinsic political and moral dimensions of everyday actions. This means teaching a moral language that is practical and meaningful in the 21st century.

**Dilemmas at school**

Here are some real examples of dilemmas put forward by primary and secondary pupils:

- 'Me and my friends always play in one corner of the playground. Some boys use our bit now just to tease. What should we do?'

- 'I saw my best friend cheating in school, shall I tell on her or not?'

- 'Someone had thrown a pencil at the display board. No

one owned up. Shall I say that I have done it (although I haven't), otherwise we won't go to the theatre?'

- 'I broke up a relationship with a girl when I was 13, because she was bullied (because I was 3 years younger than her). I did it for her, but I loved her and still do and I am not sure I did the right thing.'

At first sight a teacher's weekly selection of the football team might seem straightforward. If she selects the best players, the team is more likely to win and that is good both for the players and for the school. But that means the keen players that may be younger or not as good will miss out. In all other areas of the curriculum teachers are keen to include the less able, so why not in sports? One teacher brought this up during a *Dilemma Training* session. The teachers and assistants decided to focus on whether the school should or shouldn't have a competitive football team.

They were amazed by the quantity and quality of reasons and arguments that ended up on the flipchart during Step 4:

| The school should have a competitive football team, because | The school should not have a competitive football team, because |
|---|---|
| 1. All children have the right to have access to such opportunities | a. it is demoralising for the children not chosen; bad for their self-esteem |
| 2. Some children will have the opportunity to shine/promoting skills of the able child | b. all children should have equal opportunities |
| 3. It teaches winning/loosing skills/fair play/empathy etc | c. children might get bullied if not chosen |
| 4. It offers opportunities for the child to represent the school | d. legitimises aggressive behaviour |
| 5. Good preparation for secondary school | e. we shouldn't use competition to motivate |

| | |
|---|---|
| 6. There might be a 'Henry' in the school i.e. talent might remain unspotted otherwise! | f. it reinforces that there are only winners/losers |
| 7. It helps to develop football skills more than if it were non-competitive | g. it isolates some children |
| 8. Good publicity for the school if the football team does well | h. children not picked will get worse, because they can't progress like the others who are regularly chosen for the team |
| 9. It might attract children to the school | i) the main purpose of sports in school should be to encourage health and fitness and enjoyment for all |
| 10. It might be inspiring for people watching the games | j) including pupils who want to play even if they are not very good will promote their self-esteem |
| 11. It is more fun if the games are 'for real' | k) At primary school inclusion is more important than competitive excellence |
| 12. Provides role models of success to show what can happen if you push yourself to excel | l) Team created inclusively promotes the value of participation, rather than winning |
| 13. Gives all pupils a sense of pride in the school's achievements | m) at primary school, all children should have the experience of being in a team in order to learn cooperation and collaboration |
| 14. For the footballing champion who is no good at anything else it raises self-esteem | |
| 15. Competitive sports often motivates parents to get involved in coaching and supporting the team | |
| 16. School teams are an important part of the school's identity, so it is vital to build them to be successful – always losing is bad for morale | |

The moral strength of the various reasons was subsequently explored in step 5 of the training. By step 6 several had changed their minds on the basis of reasons they hadn't considered before. Others still believed their original decision in step 1 hadn't changed, but on the basis of new arguments had changed the reasons they would use to justify their decisions to the children, their parents and others.

## Right vs right dilemmas

In their personal and professional lives, young and old alike come up against rules and laws that seem unfair, contradictory, inappropriate or anachronistic. Confronting dilemmas that seem irresolvable can even affect mental and physical well-being. There often seems to be no means to change the situation. The response is often to try to avoid the issue, or, in more extreme cases, to take time off.

Dilemmas can come from many directions – from multi-cultural issues, sharing of resources, the sacking or disciplining of a teacher, fraud and so on. They also include bullying and child protection issues. Young people are faced with moral decisions in their capacity as family members, carers, community members and in their relationships with their peers, particularly in school and social situations as they grow in independence.

Teachers too have to make difficult decisions, for example, concerning the care and safety of students, in their assessment and testing roles, and in balancing the different educational needs of pupils. For teachers, the dilemmas are also connected with their relationships to each other, to school managers, parents and students. In the case of pupils, dilemmas are mostly connected to their relationships with each other and with their teachers. Such decisions are often made in conditions of huge pressure from management, parents and the wider public.

Here are some examples:

- 'Do I allow my pupils to discuss sensitive issues such as religion, because this might upset some parents?'

- 'I have been asked for a date by the father of one of my pupils. He is very attractive and divorced. Shall I say yes or not?'

- 'At an outdoor residential I climbed into a tree with an autistic child and stayed there to start to build a relationship with him. I am not allowed to work on 1:1 basis. Did I do the right thing?'

- Head teacher: 'A member of my team is underperforming. I suspect he has a drink problem. He has been working for our organisation for 30 years. He is 62. Shall I make him redundant or not?'

- Outdoor educator: 'There are only 10 places on an outdoor residential. I have 20 kids. Who do I choose – the ones who need it most because their behaviour has been so bad, or those who have made a real effort to be good?'

Teachers and lecturers, as with all government employees, have a special duty to act morally. A society which has no trust in its civil servants would soon disintegrate. The support *Dilemma Training* offers is not only helpful for transparency, but also for accountability.

It also has an important role to play in higher education and at management level in school and other educational institutions.

Here are some examples from higher education:

- 'Should I tell my colleagues that some students have

called them racist when I have interviewed them as part of my research, when I have assured the participants that the interviews are confidential?'

- 'A normally studious student has plagiarised an essay. Do I report her or not?'

- 'The governors of the university are discussing the future location of the faculty and there are protest posters displayed all over the campus. Should I ask staff to remove these posters during the induction week, when new students are just beginning their courses?'

- 'The faculty has been offered a large grant to take part in a curriculum development and research project. This will involve several staff and probably lead to publications and further funding. The funding body wants to have editorial control over any publications based on the research element of the project. Should we go ahead with this?'

**Six-steps training**

The six-step *Dilemma Training* method focuses on *actions.* The collaborative process helps to identify the values embedded in dilemmas and offers a practical ethical decision-making tool.

The idea, from Professor Henk van Luijk at University of Nyenrode in the Netherlands, has been extensively adapted into a tactile and visual educational resource by DialogueWorks in Britain. The metaphor of a magnifying glass is useful here. Each step is 'magnified' and 'slowed down in time'. You are 'ethically fit', when your on-the-spot decisions are similar to 'stretched-in-time' decisions.

Students not only make better ethical decisions, but they also become more aware of the ethical dimensions of what they previously thought were just practical or private decisions.

Examples of starting points:

- an eight year old lied to her teacher about homework that hadn't been done – 'but we are at school for six hours every day, isn't that enough?'.

- 'after school my neighbour is picking me up, but my mum didn't tell me this morning. Should I go with him or not?'

The method helps each person involved to solve their own selected case-studies.

Case-studies are not essential. You can also use carefully selected dilemmas from the media and other resources such as novels.

Literature can provide a rich source of starting points. For example, Peter and Renata Singer's collection *The Moral of the Story* is highly suited to secondary pupils, as are carefully selected picture books at primary level, such as *The Last Noo-Noo* by Jill Murphy, or various stories by Max Velthuijs and other authors (see References & Further Reading). The story is stopped at crucial points where a decision needs to be taken and the class is invited to think through the options.

Dilemmas from literature are often preferable to personal dilemmas, as it can take a long time to make the environment 'safe' from a group-dynamical point of view. With certain age groups, personal dilemmas can be too close for comfort. This is particularly true of teenagers. There may be cultural differences too. It could also be argued that authors of fiction have a capacity to engage the reader emotionally in ways that case-studies cannot. In the case of picture books, the interdependence between the visual images and texts is another advantage of literature over case-studies.

As part of a larger integrity programme, the training starts by listening to the dilemmas of everyone in an organisation or community as the starting point for the negotiation of new rules or codes of conduct. The training teaches people to identify the moral complexity of a dilemma, and to enrich the conversation with your inner voice before making a decision. It is a profound exercise in empathy and moral imagination.

**Benefits of the training**

The benefits of *Dilemma Training* for students, (head)teachers, parents, and others dealing with young people:

- It offers a thinking tool to distinguish right from wrong and helps to decide what to do (and make it a better decision)

- Children learn to give reasons (responsibility) and to find reasons (accountability) for what they believe and do

- It encourages empathy and inner dialogue (therefore critical & creative thinking)

- They learn to think before they act

- They are encouraged to think for themselves (with the help of others) – basic speaking & listening skills are enhanced

- Makes them more confident in believing what is 'right' (develops a strong sense of self)

- Helps them to resist peer pressure when necessary (independent thinking)

- Exposes the core-dilemmas of an educational organisation

- Offers opportunities to really listen to young people

- Helps to develop rules and ethical codes that are based on young people's concrete everyday experiences

- Young people feel valued, and experience that what they say and think can make a real difference

- Enriches citizenship education, Personal Social Health Education and peer tutoring.

**To tell, or not to tell – The dilemma**

In business or politics it is called 'whistleblowing'. In the playground it is 'grassing up your mates'. Whatever the terminology and whatever the context, exposing wrongdoing usually carries huge risks. The stakes can be frighteningly high, and the courage involved is immense. Considering the pressures involved, how do children choose between telling the truth about something they think is wrong, and being loyal to their classmates?

Loyalty and truth are important values – equally important. Telling the truth is an integral part of 'honesty' which is regarded as one of the most important virtues, and a cornerstone of a person's integrity. How can a young person decide which action to take when both courses of action – telling and not telling – are the right thing to do?

A west Wales primary school is believed to be the world's first to have trained its students in ethical decision making. The school's 8 to 10-year-olds have been taught to decide for themselves the morally correct course of action when faced with difficult choices. On the first day of training, the students at Manorbier School, Pembrokeshire, chose the dilemma, 'If I'm bullied should I tell Miss?'. Their arguments are listed below. Subsequently in Step 5 they assessed the moral strength of an argument.

It is helpful to teach the distinction between *principles* and *consequences*.

Consequences are about what happens next. Often this means getting into trouble, getting money, or being told off. They can be about personal gain, avoiding trouble, and are usually tangible. Principles are to do with what most people think is fundamentally good, bad, right or wrong, such as stealing or telling tales. They are often about violating rights. Identifying principles or consequences is not always easy.

Sometimes, consequential arguments presuppose a principle. Take, for example, argument 10 below. It is morally right to tell the teacher because it might help you relieve stress. The consequence is stress reduction, but the underlying principle is 'care for the health of an individual'. The lack of a mathematical sort of certainty in assessing the arguments might bother some, but what really matters is the enquiry it provokes in the classroom or staffroom.

Participants have to critically reflect on their own thinking and take a more objective stance when assessing the arguments. Also, thinking together about the arguments sometimes reveals they weren't real arguments in the first place. For example, in c. a solution is offered that is not an argument for or against telling the teacher – similarly in the case of f..

After working in small groups and reflecting on the columns themselves the trainer went through each argument and judged collaboratively whether consequences or principles were involved and why.

| Tell the teacher<br>Because | Don't tell the teacher<br>Because |
|---|---|
| 1. she can give a solution, because talking might not be possible<br>Consequence (C) | a. you can do it your own way by talking about it<br>Principle (P) Autonomy |
| 2. it could scare them<br>(C) | b. you don't grass on people<br>(P) Loyalty (not betraying others) |
| 3. if it is really serious or you are really scared it keeps you away from the bullies<br>(C)<br>(P) Right to protection (safety) | c. you have cousins/relatives to sort it out |
| 4. you could move schools then<br>(C) | d. the teacher might do something about it and you don't want that because you be friends again tomorrow<br>(P) Autonomy (sorting own problems out) |
| 5. you sometimes want to tell the truth<br>(P) Honesty | e. you might have learnt that you should fight your own battles (eg parents)<br>(P) Autonomy |
| 6. they wouldn't stop<br>(C)<br>(P) Right to protection | f. you always have a choice |
| 7. it's the teacher's job to keep you safe<br>(P) Safety | g. they say 'stop telling tales' (C) |
| 8. it helps you to concentrate without all of that on your mind<br>(C)<br>(P) Right to a good education | h. they call you a 'chicken'<br>(C) |
| 9. it is the teacher's responsibility to help you get a better future (eg jobs)<br>(P) Right to a good education<br>(C) | i. they bully you even more<br>(C)<br>(P) Care for Self |

| | |
|---|---|
| 10. they might help you with stress (C) (P) Care for self (own health) | j. they don't do anything about it (C) |
| 11. teacher should know (P) Right to information | k. teachers can't heal you teachers can't keep you safe all the time (P) Autonomy |
| 12. things can change because it wouldn't be fair for <u>me</u> to move schools (P) Fairness | l. it's not teacher's business (P) Autonomy |

Quite a few had changed their mind, but not the example giver, although his reasons for going to the teacher, and also his initial decision, had changed. He hadn't thought of the argument that it could be the teacher's job to protect him. The class was more or less split in half, which showed how much of a real dilemma it was.

The conflicting values were *right to protection, education* and *honesty* (fairness was important only for one person) pulling in the direction of telling the teacher, and *autonomy* and *loyalty* pulling in the other direction – as is typical of a right versus right dilemma. Whatever you choose, there is always a moral cost. What is worth mentioning is that *care for self* is on both sides, which is often the case in a genuine dilemma.

All children could now give reasons for their decisions and all felt reasonably good about them.

This analysis clearly shows how it is sometimes inappropriate for adults to get involved in bullying issues. Despite the fact that the relationship with their teacher is very good – hence the fact that *honesty* played such an important role for them – and that the school offers a caring learning environment, there are occasions when the children wanted to sort out these issues for themselves. Introduction of peer mentoring could be a way of avoiding such dilemmas.

## What did the school think of the training?

The headteacher acknowledged that the training is an excellent tool for helping children to deal with any dilemmas that may face them, including those connected to difficult issues such as substance abuse (see Chapter 11).

She had been surprised that bullying had been brought up as a dilemma, as the school prided itself in having an effective anti-bullying policy. Yet when the training threw up bullying as a topic the children offered a plethora of ideas, issues and creative solutions.

Because they deal with dilemmas by thinking for themselves within a group, the children also show an unusual level of respect for each other's opinions and differences, and surprising levels of empathy. The school will use this in the knowledge that it will empower the students further, enabling them to make much more informed choices in the future.

## What next?

The first step is to train the school staff to teach the ethical decision-making process. For some schools this directly connects with the curriculum, in particular Personal and Social Education, Citizenship, and Religious Education. But there are also more indirect links with science and the humanities.

On the basis that good decision making is central to citizenship and personal and social education, the Welsh Assembly (Wales' regional government) has also endorsed *Dilemma Training* for primary schools by awarding Cwrt-Yr-Ala Junior School in Cardiff a substantial innovation grant to create a school council based on 'communities of enquiry'.

The school's *Council for Good Judgement* project engaged children, teachers, parents and governors in transforming the traditional idea of the school council into a more reflective think tank. The project programme included *Dilemma Training* and *Philosophy with Children.*

These two approaches were chosen because they create the thoughtful and open-minded dispositions the project aimed to achieve. It was felt that this would promote moral integrity, and that the acquired practical wisdom would continue to benefit the children for a long time afterwards.

**Ways out of the moral maze**

A return to external authority gives little practical moral guidance for deciding between different courses of action, especially when it is not just a matter of choosing between right or wrong, but between two *right* courses of action.

With the rejection of traditional moral guidance, teachers need to invest in innovative, creative ways of educating people to find their own reasoned way out of the moral maze. In an 'anything goes' era most feel uncomfortable with expressing their own beliefs about what is right and wrong – afraid of being accused of being bigots. Reminding people of their moral responsibility is unpopular, boring, not 'cool' and often met with a 'we agree to disagree' response. It is therefore all the more essential to create space for people to explore the rights and wrongs of certain actions by critically examining each others' reasons for them.

The time is right for key national institutions to put their weight behind a new open and democratic process that will offer support, not just for young people, but for everyone. All are in 'the same boat'. At present, moral demands are excitingly unique and we need urgent guidance and support for learning how to make better moral decisions on a day-to-day basis.

Fortunately, most people have an intuitive feeling of the difference between right and wrong and base their actions on implicit values and principles, even when they are not aware of them. Some people call it 'conscience' or 'inner voice'. But conscience can be educated and our inner conversation – the conversation we have with ourselves before we make a difficult decision – can be informed, enriched and expanded.

**It is likely that if young children are trained in ethical decision-making they are less likely to get caught up in private and professional structures that prevent them from behaving ethically. This is because it helps give them the courage to stand up for themselves, and to make the choices they believe are morally right. The younger they start the better.**

# 11

## SUBSTANCE ABUSE – SAYING 'NO!'

Anyone who can say 'no!' to drugs is not an addict. An addict needs to acquire the means to say 'no' – and then is an addict no longer.

Whether you are an 'addict' or not, any habit is harmful to yourself and others when it exceeds the level compatible with ethical conduct. It is at that point that it becomes *abuse*. Examples include excessive consumption of alcohol, drugs, tobacco, food (binge eating), or dieting (anorexia).

Gaining control over the use of substances depends on acquiring the means to *choose* whether to continue with the habit, to moderate it or to give it up. Such a choice depends on the ability to make rational *decisions*.

**Don't say 'Don't'**

Simply telling young people 'don't use drugs' rarely succeeds, and can be counter-productive. They are more likely to take notice when the message respects their ability to make their own decisions.

This assumes that they are capable of doing so. However, some people lack the key intellectual, social, or moral resources they need to decide to stop. They fail to think before they act. They might fail to realise the effect their habit is having on other people. They may also fail to reflect back on the consequences of their actions. In which case, even punishment wouldn't necessarily help.

The solution is to acquire and *internalise* a decision-making process so that they can *decide for themselves* whether or not to break the habit.

Also, because we need *autonomous* decision making when confronted with any dilemmas and any choices in life, such habits of thought will support ethical behaviour in all walks of life.

**Four levels from temptation to abuse**

There are four basic levels of the use of stimulants. They are the temptation to use substances, the actual use of substances, *mis*use of substances, and addiction.

*Dilemma Training* plays a role in the first three:

• Temptation: where young people are tempted to experiment with stimulants such as alcohol, and soft and hard drugs, or are tempted to relapse after recovering from addiction.

• Using substances: where youngsters and adults regularly use substances, but where there is not necessarily misuse or addiction.

- Misuse: where there is misuse, or a strong possibility of misuse, and where there are consequences for self and others.

The training also helps in situations where others are confronted with the consequences of use, misuse, or addiction, such as parents, family, police, teachers, youth workers, and children of parents that are users. These are often accompanied by difficult moral choices governed by reactions as diverse as guilt, anger and good intentions.

Drawing on the capacity of people for self-help, the training takes seriously what young people themselves think about substance misuse. Exchanging ideas and experiences produces choices that are better informed.

*Dilemma Training* complements the usual medical model of understanding and dealing with addiction. Whilst substance misuse is a problem in itself, it is often also a response to other problems such as poverty or not being loved or valued.

The training challenges the idea that dependence can be explained merely as a physiological process in which the addict has no free will. One counter example is a user who gave up heroin as soon as she found she was pregnant – but then started again after giving birth!

A full programme would consist of:

- building *communities of moral enquiry* in which individuals in a group learn to take *responsibility* for their own and the group's behaviour and decisions. Such groups include users, families, carers, and other community members. Members of a group who are taken seriously without giving way to peer pressure gain enormously in self-esteem and confidence in their own decisions.

- *Dilemma Training* to strengthen an individual's moral reasoning. This process, which involves peer tutoring, strengthens individual moral judgement through group dialogue enabling each participant to recognise the right action in their own everyday lives, and to justify an answer to the question 'Is what I am doing morally right?'. They also gain insight into their basic dilemmas.

- *Socratic dialogues* explore the core values implied in these dilemmas and help to develop democratically the new rules and codes of conduct.

- *Outdoor residential weekends* as powerful starting points for ethical enquiries with selected groups of young people at risk.

## Drugs prevention programmes

Drugs prevention programmes have a long history. Numerous interventions have been developed during the past three decades in western countries. Some of these are carried out in schools. Some are aimed at parents of teenagers and professionals from drugs prevention agencies. Most aim at young people aged 10-16 in the hope of reaching them before they have started to use drugs.

Traditionally, preventative interventions are divided into three categories:

- *Primary*: to prevent substance misuse and dependency disorders.

- *Secondary*: to catch people who have only recently started substance misuse.

- *Tertiary*: therapy to limit the damage caused by substance misuse.

More recently-developed preventative interventions include:

- *Universal*: aimed at all or part of a particular social group selected according to certain risk factors (e.g., media campaigns and programmes for a whole school).

- *Selective*: for individuals and groups that have a higher risk of substance misuse (e.g., programmes for children of alcoholics or for young people in particular areas).

- *Indicated*: for people who have not got an addiction problem according to the usual diagnostic criteria, but who nonetheless show signs of misuse (e.g., interventions aimed at young people who experiment with substances).

- *Early* interventions: aimed at people who have addiction problems according to the usual diagnostic criteria, but who have not yet sought help.

*Dilemma Training* can best be regarded as a *primary intervention programme* suited to *all preventative interventions*.

If young people are to make ethical decisions, the adults and other young people around them need to do so too.

The main focus is not the drug user or the 'problem kid' – though certain young people 'at risk' do get special attention in residentials – but on creating a more ethical community for everyone.

The basic idea is that the root lies in creating an environment where people can think critically and morally about substance misuse. It is the creation of such an environment or community that plays a crucial role in the possibility of making autonomous, considered, and morally correct decisions.

Youngsters and trainers participate in small groups seeking better understanding of each other's ways of thinking and feeling about various issues. The community aspect is central. By discussing ethical issues such as fundamental questions about right and wrong, freedom and responsibility, participants are encouraged to listen to and reason with each other. This helps to generate mutual respect.

## *Mind & Muscle*

The aim of outdoor residentials is to provide education with recreation. Participants take part in various outdoor pursuits, and then are asked to reflect on the thoughts and feelings these generate. This helps develop essential personal and social skills based on thinking, communicating, and taking action.

In the outdoor *'Muscle'* part of the programme, participants experience the natural environment, which, given its difference from home or school, demands adaptation and risk taking. They also experience the excitement of being able to lose themselves completely in an endeavour. This is explicitly tied to intrinsic motivation.

It encourages teamwork, cooperation, trust, and responsibility for personal safety. Creating opportunities to build confidence and self-esteem, it also offers the experience of a simpler, healthier and non-commercialised existence. It gives time to reflect – to put life into perspective and reconsider attitudes and values.

During the indoor *'Mind'* part of the programme – critical reflection, thinking, and enquiry – participants examine the various causes of substance abuse and offending behaviour. This helps to improve cognitive skills and moral reasoning.

Poor *Cognitive skills* can be reflected in:

• inability to understand other people;

- impulsivity and lack of self-control;

- lack of ability to reappraise new situations;

- believing that they have little control over their lives – that what happens is beyond their control and merely the result of external influences;

- inability to empathise;

- poor interpersonal skills, including *a lack of*:

  > ability to get situations in perspective;
  > skills in interpreting non-verbal communication;
  > sensitivity to recognise the potential problems when people interact;
  > ability to generate alternative solutions, and to consider the consequences for themselves and others;
  > understanding the effect they have on other people's behaviour.

The outdoor residentials use continuous reviewing and self-assessment to help secure a lasting transfer of what has been learned to the participants' everyday lives. The legacy of experiencing 'external' dialogue is to support future 'internal' dialogue.

**Whatever prevention, rehabilitation, punishment, or placement schemes are tried with young abusers, the fundamental challenge remains:** *to help people to develop their own resources to make and sustain the decision to say 'no!' to substance abuse.*

I know you
love me,

but you must
let me go. X

# 12

# TOBACCO DOESN'T KILL; SMOKING KILLS

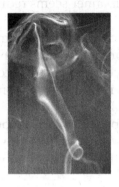

---

*'The TMA defends the legitimate interests of its member companies and the freedom of adults to make an informed choice about whether to smoke or not.'*

*The Tobacco Manufacturers' Association, London.*

---

It's not only users who can benefit from *Dilemma Training*. The producers and pushers of substances could equally benefit from asking themselves 'is what I am doing morally right?' This also applies to those involved in legal drugs, such as tobacco.

Sceptics who already regard 'business ethics' as a contradiction in terms, would be horrified at finding 'ethics' and 'tobacco' in the same sentence. Often regarded as worse even than the arms trade, tobacco is seen as the world's sin industry *par excellence*.

Even the most ethically myopic would probably accept that obstacles to ethical behaviour for tobacco producers are insurmountable. It is not just their conduct that attracts censure but their very existence – their *raison d'être* being to produce a drug that quickly hooks their customers and slowly kills them.

Criticism focuses not just on the nature of the product, but also on the conduct of the companies. Given that they admit that cigarettes pose a real health risk but will not stop making them, the question of whether they can behave in a socially responsible manner seems redundant.

Some of the public's concerns are common to all industries. These include environmental, health and safety impact, fair treatment of employees, customers, commercial partners, and other stakeholders in the wider community.

Other concerns are specific to tobacco products. The serious and real health risks associated with smoking distinguish tobacco from most other consumer goods.

The industry's arguments in favour of its continued existence vary from pragmatic to sheer sophistry. They are that:

- tobacco products are among the most highly regulated products in the US and Europe, and are one of the most highly taxed.

- even accepting that cigarette production is unethical, the demand for cigarettes is enormous; and that if cigarettes were to be withdrawn this would prohibit people from making their own choice. The situation, they say, would be much like the alcohol prohibition of the 1920s.

- tobacco is a legal product and millions of informed people choose to smoke, despite knowing the health risks, and would probably do so even if their government banned tobacco.

- the tobacco companies say that if any one of them did not manufacture cigarettes, someone else would.

Having claimed to have established a right to exist, it would seem sensible for a cigarette maker to convince its stakeholders that they will strive to be as good a corporate citizen as possible. That is why there has been a spate of Corporate Social Responsibility (CSR) reports and codes of conduct coming from the major tobacco manufacturers.

They say they see their challenges as:

- given the dangerous nature of their products, supporting developments relating to smoking and health, to fund independent research studying the dangers of tobacco products, and what might be done to make them less dangerous.

- limiting their marketing to adult consumers who choose to smoke. Marketing practices should not encourage smoking among the young, or among non-smokers. (This is a bitter pill to swallow because it is committing itself to reducing the size of its future customer base.)

- dealing with the issues surrounding public smoking and environmental tobacco smoke by encouraging the use of smoking-free areas in public places.

- demonstrating good corporate citizenship by using resources to meet the needs of the community – ranging from traditional philanthropy to community volunteerism.

- ensuring suppliers respect the industry's core values. This is especially important in the case of labour conditions and use of child labour.

- making it easier for whistleblowers to address issues.

Anti-smoking campaigners say that the new image and claims of corporate citizenship are a shallow public relations whitewash.

But if it is accepted that, because the tobacco industry is so powerful and so important as a source of revenue to governments, it is here to stay, it makes sense to encourage its ethical behaviour through the various channels available, rather than pressing for its total annihilation.

It is therefore in the interests of both the industry and society to ensure best practice in all aspects of its business conduct and, in particular, that it works to reduce the health impact of tobacco products to existing smokers, to discourage its use among young people, and expansion of its consumption generally. This would mean that expansion of market share would have to be at the expense of competitors, and competitiveness would be on the basis of offering a less dangerous product.

From an 'ethicist's' point of view, the issue of smoking raises a lot of issues concerning a variety of values. 'Freedom of choice' is often emphasised by those in favour of smoking, although even the most ardent supporters of liberty are inclined to acknowledge that liberty can be restricted in areas where harm would otherwise result. This is why the issue of what harm smoking actually causes is so important.

However, as the tobacco industry can also point out, such activities as boxing are intrinsically harmful, yet our society rests content with regulating them rather than banning them, and admits the pursuit of them as acceptable choices.

In its defence, the tobacco industry might also want to emphasise the parallels with alcohol. Tobacco rarely makes people beat their wives or kill people through reckless driving.

On the other hand, these 'arguments' look like excuses of the 'everybody does it' variety.

Is banning tobacco on the same level as banning guns? A favourite slogan of the pro-gun lobby in the USA is 'Guns don't kill, people do'. So there is a question of where responsibility is to be located. Is the creation (or, in this case, processing) of something harmful wrong in itself?

To parody the slogan of the US National Rifle Association, 'tobacco doesn't kill – smoking kills', blaming the tobacco companies for death and illness due to smoking ignores the element of personal responsibility involved. It verges on patronising.

People still have a choice – the choice to say 'no' to smoking. Such a choice depends on the ability to make *decisions*.

**This depends on acquiring and *internalising* a decision-making process which takes account of the rights and wishes, not only of the decision maker, but also of other stakeholders involved, such as the general public, the health service, friends and family.**

# 13

## AMSTERDAM

## EMBRACES DILEMMA TRAINING

The Dutch parliament has passed legislation compelling ministries and local governments to draw up and implement an 'integrity' policy. The policy consists of prevention and cure – training in *right action* backed up by the possibility of crime detection and punishment.

The preventative side of the integrity policy consists of training civil servants and council workers in ethical decision making, ongoing advice and coaching, and a forum in which employees can discuss the training and use their experiences to formulate basic moral values.

Amsterdam has long had the reputation of being one of the world's most anarchic cities. Vibrant with nightlife, art and music, and a melting-pot for cultures from most parts of the world, the city has long regarded itself as unmanageable. The city council claims that all this is changing tiny step by tiny step. In the past few years it has been more successful in managing the unmanageable, has cracked down heavily on organised crime, and has turned its attention to itself.

With a population of only three quarters of a million, Amsterdam is decentralised into 15 boroughs and 40 departments such as sanitation, fire, buildings inspection, run by its 22,000 council workers. Presiding over all of this are the mayor and his eight aldermen.

In September 2001, at the mayor Job Cohen's request, the council set up its Integrity Bureau (*Bureau Integriteit*) to investigate and prevent corruption within the council, its boroughs, and services. It has a full-time staff of 15.

Not that the city fathers were convinced that their city was corrupt to the core. On the contrary. A report in the late 1990s – *Correct or Corrupt* – concluded that by and large the city's workers were 'clean'. But, particularly in planning and buildings inspection, there was considerable room for improvement.

Granting planning permission, putting major public works out to tender, and agreeing subsidies are just a few of the day-to-day decisions for many of the council's workers. The temptations to influence these decisions for personal gain can be huge. But cases of misconduct were seen as exceptions. The council simply decided to demonstrate to its citizens that it has an open, just, and democratic local government.

This is no easy task. Modern day integrity depends on the ability to make ethical decisions individually, without reference to an authority such as the State or Church. This was clearly going to severely stretch councillors, civil servants, and council workers. It involved not only big issues such as racism and bribery, but also the sort of dilemmas faced by ordinary people every day in their workplace.

Against this backcloth, almost immediately after founding the Integrity Bureau, the council brought in the services of Dutch ethicists Governance & Integrity (G&I). Their training neatly complements the Bureau's prevention side. Its 'curative' side still relies on investigators and lawyers. The link between the two is a team that carries out integrity risk analyses either as the result of a tip-off about misconduct, or at the request of a borough to examine its vulnerability to corruption. The analysis reports always recommend integrity training.

On the preventative side all council staff are given *Dilemma Training*, starting with the management team in the boroughs and service departments. They will also assist in ongoing management of integrity through advice and coaching, and development of a *community of moral enquiry* in which employees can discuss the dilemmas arising from the training, use them to formulate basic moral values, and use these to form the basis of rules of conduct.

## The Integrity Bureau

---

*'Some civil servants don't seem to realise they're working with public money. They sometimes act as though they're spending their own!'*

*Fergal van de Wouw, director of legal affairs, Integrity Bureau, Amsterdam City Council.*

---

The bare, grey, cubic council building which houses the Integrity Bureau's offices, appropriately overlooks the leafy Spinoza Street on the other side of the Singel canal. This is where the 17th century philosopher Spinoza incarcerated himself to write his famous *Ethics*, published in 1677.

Amsterdam was just as rebellious in Spinoza's day. The Dutch had shaken off the tyranny of the Austrians and the Spanish, and of Church and State. The new merchant class rose to dominate life in an atmosphere of relative tolerance towards different cultures and faiths. That tolerance has remained a feature of the city ever since. But by the late 20th century it had allowed organised crime to get a strong foothold in drugs and prostitution.

'There has been a time of almost *anything goes*,' comments Heleen de Koningh, Integrity Bureau's acting director. 'That is slowly changing, and the establishment of this bureau partly reflects that change.'

The bureau started in the aftermath of several scandals in Amsterdam in the mid-1990s. As is usually the case, the initial reaction was repressive – sending in investigators and punishing wrongdoers, but council misconduct is not a priority for the police and public prosecutors. 'That left us with the need to set up an internal bureau to deal with local government corruption,' says de Koningh. Prevention is better than cure, and we have both.'

Amsterdam City Council has stated the belief that Dutch citizens have the right to a local government they can trust. The Council decided this would be done through a programme to internalise ethical behaviour, rather than only through codes of conduct, and that every council member and worker would be given the skills necessary to making a moral judgement – to answering the question '*Is what I do morally right?*'

Heleen de Koningh points out that it's not just about accepting gifts or how much you can spend on dinners. It's all about the real, everyday dilemmas that occur in your own workplace. For example, problems with firing staff – perhaps you like them, or don't want to upset the other staff – or how to deal with people taking files home for their own professional research.

Any fraud or corruption is a serious problem, but the bureau uses the training as a method that teases out the real dilemmas found in the workplace, which can be applied to any ethical decision making. The bureau believes that dilemmas – such as whether or not to blow the whistle – cannot be dealt with adequately by a code of conduct because those involved are often not even aware of the dilemmas at the root of the decision they are faced with. This is often made worse by the fact that managers don't always come out of the profession itself, so referring to the boss is not always the best solution. He or she might not be equipped to deal with it.

*Dilemma Training* at the heart of an integrity package gives staff members a new insight into different facets of dilemmas, and empowers them with the right tools to express the fundamental issues at stake. It puts the responsibility and the capacity squarely on the shoulders of the staff member with the dilemma, rather than leaving them to refer to another authority, be it the line manager or a code of conduct.

## Does it work?

But does it work? The bureau is still young, so there are no statistics on its effectiveness. And it's questionable whether it will ever be able to measure effectiveness statistically. Even if it could somehow measure integrity among its 22,000 workers it would never be able to strip out the possible effect of social change – of people becoming more moral in general.

What most impressed the politicians at the top was the training itself, which they all undertook as part of the top-down approach. They were particularly impressed by the changes in the way that staff now approach problem solving and discussion of difficult issues, particularly their ability to view complicated issues from various angles, and to appreciate different perspectives.

Several issues that were previously taboo have now become subjects of open discussion. These include, for example, issues surrounding racial equality, perceived slacking by colleagues, various collegial problems, loyalty, and fraud.

Asking the question *'Is this morally correct?'* is now quite usual among council workers. Management has raised its commitment to integrity, and there has been an increase in tip-offs about violations, due not to a decline in integrity, but to an enhanced awareness of integrity issues, and an increased desire to deal with them.

Fergal van de Wouw, head of the bureau's legal affairs department, accepts the difficulty in measuring an improvement in integrity. 'I think that the bottom line is simply *can your workers stand up to scrutiny?'*, he concludes. 'Can they explain their actions, and morally justify them? If your staff have nothing to fear and nothing to hide, they work in a more relaxed manner, they get on better with each other, they work more efficiently, and they probably take less sick leave.'

**Who does it?**

As the result of the bureau's integrity risk analysis, managers are advised on how to deal with those risks and reduce them, perhaps by changes to organisational procedures. They are enthusiastic about the results, which have given them an effective tool to help solve various ethical problems.

It is up to the directors of each of Amsterdam's boroughs and departments to decide whether to adopt the integrity training, and at which level it will be applied. Usually, it is compulsory for all of employees.

The greatest resistance to the training comes from lawyers, says Heleen de Koningh. 'Lawyers nearly always focus on rules. They seem to think that the whole world is, or can be, organised in rules, and that therefore you don't need integrity training. Then you have to explain to them that personal relationships, including in the workplace, cannot be covered by rules, and furthermore, that rules are nearly always reactive – after the events they are supposed to control. They never quite catch up. And people are amazingly clever at circumventing them.'

## Centralising data

Decentralisation of Amsterdam's municipality undermined any attempt at an overview of the extent of fraud and corruption. To counter this, the city set up its Central Fraud and Corruption Register (*Centraal Registratiepunt Integriteits Schendingen*). As well as registering all reported cases of fraud it advises and supports council efforts to combat corruption, facilitates contact with the police, and provides legal advice.

All bureau cases are filed with the city's Central Fraud and Corruption Register. Although the data can be used to plot trends, it is rarely of any use to draw firm conclusions.

Any public organisation that has started its own investigation into misconduct is obliged to inform the bureau, which passes the information to the central register. A significant problem is that those who come clean about their cases in-house are often slaughtered by the press, while those who keep quiet avoid bad publicity. In the case of firms claiming to have no cases of corruption, the bureau interviews them and gets them to explain how it is possible that they have no such problems.

## Analysis – Prevention and cure

---

*'We are setting an example, and other councils will follow suit. We are lucky to have a mayor of exceptional intelligence and integrity. I just hope that future mayors will be smart enough to appreciate the benefits. But since politicians have only a four-year horizon, who knows what's gonna happen. We take it one assignment at a time with the idea that any is a lot better than none.'*

*Rosemarijn van der Meij, Director of Risk Analysis, Integrity Bureau, Amsterdam City Council.*

---

Prevention is better than cure. The bulk of Integrity Bureau risk analyses are now triggered by pro-active requests by a borough or local government department, rather than as the result of tip-offs about existing corruption.

'This is more than just about dealing with backhanders,' says the bureau's director of risk analysis, Rosemarijn van der Meij. 'It's about understanding different points of view, and being able to discuss moral issues in a reasonable way with your colleagues. It can have an immense team-building effect which is simply inspiring.'

The bureau carries out a risk analysis of all of Amsterdam's boroughs. Most have already highlighted areas such as waste disposal and sanitation departments, building and housing inspectorates, and tendering for public works that are most vulnerable to corruption.

As a natural step forward after the analysis, the assessment always recommends integrity training as part of a preventative package. Van der Meij points out that the training significantly helps deal with staff who are involved in having to change procedures as the result of the risk analysis. They are much more capable and willing to see the different perspectives involved in accepting the need for change. Furthermore, an important aspect of the training is that the dilemmas that arise during the sessions can themselves signpost areas vulnerable to misconduct. In other words, the training itself can complement the analysis.

The bureau's experience has been that if it applies the training after the risk analysis there is no resistance by staff members. This is because the analysis helps people see clearly that certain procedures are vulnerable to corruption, and that the training is an effective method of preventing problems of real misconduct.

## What the managers say

Ronald Prins, who heads the Amsterdam borough of Bos en Lommer, is typical of an executive caught between a rock and a hard place. He is responsible to his political masters on the council, but also to the needs and wishes of his team of civil servants and other council workers. And now he has to deal with the council's drive to clean up the city and its public servants.

A risk analysis by the Bureau has thrown up not only areas of potential corruption, but also three areas where there are already significant corruption problems. In one of them, waste disposal, corruption by Amsterdam's 'waste mafia' has become a tradition.

The Bureau, with the full support of the mayor, has recommended *Dilemma Training* for Ronald Prins' team. It's a recommendation he really cannot ignore or he'll have to face a grilling by the council's Integrity Committee. On the other hand, he knows that his staff will complain that they're too busy, and that they have to complete so many training courses of various types that they hardly ever have time to do enough 'real work'.

However, Prins says resistance doesn't last long. He says the training is so powerful and so effective, that once people do it they immediately appreciate its benefits, word gets round, and resistance falls away.

He himself has completed the training, and found it powerfully changes the way you think about decision making. He described it as a highly systematic method that enables you to deal with almost any dilemma at work or in your private life.

And he doesn't have the problem of having to justify the time and expense to his masters. It has the complete support, and pressure even, from the mayor and aldermen down.

## Brass from muck – an inherited scam

The Bureau analyses discovered scams that have been part of local life for decades. This includes theft and resale of non-ferrous metals from the waste stream, and charging householders to collect their waste. They also take trade waste from small businesses as household waste for a fee that is less than the official tariff. And, they'll collect waste ahead of the scheduled day – for a fee.

The borough of Bos en Lommer has a high immigrant population. Only 40% is Dutch. The immigrants' expectations of local government help are coloured by experience in their country of birth. They often expect to be charged for a council service, and don't expect their complaints to be acted upon. Furthermore, complaining can cause more trouble than it is worth. Some of those that have tried have woken up to find half a tonne of rubbish piled against their front door, or have had to run a gauntlet of screaming dustmen lined up in front of their house.

Some of the waste collectors have been working these scams for decades. Some learned the trade from their fathers. There's a hierarchy among them – the winners and losers, the toughest and the less tough. They feel isolated from the rest of the community, victims even. It's 'Us and Them'. Managers cut little ice. Few of them last longer than a couple of years. They either get sacked for incompetence, or get promoted elsewhere. And firing isn't the answer. Prins says they just get replaced with others who soon get sucked into the system.

### Why *Dilemma Training?*

'Other methods we have looked at are either too philosophical, or, at the other extreme, are too practical and not sufficiently theoretical,' according to bureau chief, Heleen de Koningh. 'For us in the civil service it is also a highly practical and effective way of discovering the sorts of workplace dilemmas. The training not only consists of a method of ethical decision making, but the trainer also makes an inventory of the fundamental dilemmas arising from it, and these can be reported to the department manager who, in turn, gets a better understanding of the decisions faced by his or her staff members.'

Fergal van de Wouw in legal affairs is a firm supporter of integrity training as a preventative measure. He says it has even been effective in the bureau itself, and that it has changed the way the bureau staff themselves look at various issues from different perspectives, and how they discuss them more reasonably and effectively among each other.

**Integrity is high on the agenda because a democratic local government is seen as having a moral function in society; and it can function only with the trust of the public.**

# 14

## ETHICS IN BUSINESS
## RESOLVING THE CONTRADICTIONS

5 317738 553793 7

The claim that 'business ethics is a contradiction in terms' – an oxymoron – is a cliché. It reflects a widespread conviction that business people behave differently at work from how they would at home – that something at the heart of business makes it incompatible with the moral standards of everyday life. As soon as ordinary people put on business suits, they become immune to the moral implications of their actions, and metamorphose into profit psychopaths. Can this be true?

There are indeed people who behave very badly in order to advance their own narrowly drawn interests. But you find them in all walks of life. To blame business for the immoral behaviour of some of its practitioners is like blaming Sheffield steelmakers for a bar-room stabbing.

Business itself is not inherently bad, but the practices of some business people are sometimes morally objectionable. This is reflected in the increased levels of business crime and corruption. It does look as though too many business people are allowing values like increasing market share or maximising profits to override other values, like fair competition, care for the environment, and welfare of employees. Financial scandals involving established and trusted businesses have created the impression in the public mind that business and ethics don't mix, and that commercial pressures mean bad morals.

One thing is clear, bad moral practice cannot be the norm in business. If businesses were just a matter of dog eat dog, there would be no one to do business with. In the natural world, the redness of tooth and claw makes sense only against the background of considerable cooperation and symbiosis. A business can act ruthlessly in the horizontal direction only because, at least for most of the time, it is able to cooperate in mutually acceptable ways in vertical directions, with its suppliers and customers. If lying, betrayal, and cheating were what everyone had to do, all the time, just to stay in the game, the game itself would fall apart.

Introduction of Business Ethics as a subject is often seen as a knee-jerk reaction to business scandals. This too easily gives the impression that the purpose of reflecting on morality is to provide space for moralising – for telling managers 'Don't lie, don't steal, don't cheat'.

This goes against two common-sense moral intuitions. The first is that, for the most part, people do not need to be told such things. And second, that if people do really need to be told such things, it is highly unlikely that they will stop doing them just because ethics trainers have told them to. The point is that public outrage about business scandals is in direct proportion to their obvious violations of widely accepted moral beliefs. But the greater the outrage, the more widely accepted the moral beliefs involved. So there is little point in trying to impress them upon managers.

Ethics is usually treated as external to business activity. The view seems to be that business is essentially amoral, and so it needs to be surrounded with a set of moral constraints.

The underlying problem of treating ethics as external to business is that it means regarding the moral point of view as one among a competing set of perspectives between which the manager can choose. The manager evaluates the situation from the financial perspective, from the shareholder perspective, from the point of view of corporate marketing, from a personnel point of view. And then, we are asked to believe, having done all this, he may, if he is an ethically-aware manager, evaluate it from a moral point of view.

The debate then revolves around the question of whether there is time and justification for adding this perspective. The trouble is that where the moral perspective is conceived as just one among several equally important others, there can be a case for leaving it out altogether.

Imagine a case in which a manager can extend his business legally and without loss of reputation, but where doing so involves something morally questionable. Perhaps he is contacted by a malcontent employee of a rival firm who tells him about their proposed new product range. Should he use the information as the basis of some pre-emptive product development? Why not?

Why can't morality be put to one side as an unnecessary hindrance? Why bother with it? If moral considerations are optional, surely there is no reason to consistently include them.

The reality is not like this. It is the other, financial, political, even aesthetic perspectives, that are essentially optional. That is not to say that you do not have pressing reasons to adopt them. Jobs may depend upon it. Still, they remain perspectives you can take up or change as you think fit.

But the 'moral point of view' is not optional in this sense. It comes looking for you. In the above example, the manager cannot choose whether or not to see the moral problem. He already has the moral problem – does the character of the source of the information make it impossible to use? A manager in this situation cannot simply refuse to take up a moral perspective. It has already asserted itself.

In fact, worrying about how he might get from a business point of view to a moral point of view is about as pointless as worrying how he might get from Manhattan to New York.

Similarly, we should say that if a manager, perhaps under pressure from top management, is trying to balance the interests of shareholders, the interests of existing management, perhaps including himself, the interests of employees, and perhaps those of a wider group of stakeholders, what he has got is a moral problem, because he has to decide the priority of these interests in the total scheme of his organisation. And this is a good example of ethical decision making, taking account of the rights and wishes of relevant stakeholders.

Outrage over high profile scandals is not then the real reason for thinking about the business of ethics. Ethics is not needed in business and management courses in order to curb the future excesses of the business world. Rather, reflection on ethics should be an integral part of the management sciences because the nature of organisational management demands it. Ethical thinking is integral to the character of management thinking.

## Power to the consumers & corporate social responsibility

Companies and institutions worldwide are facing up to responsibilities that integrate social, environmental and economic interests. This reflects not only social and legislative pressures but also the recognition that new economic opportunities depend on good corporate citizenship.

Consumer power is dictating business behaviour. Western businesses are closely scrutinised by consumer pressure groups, demanding more ethical corporate management, improved environmental performance, and accountability to stakeholder groups other than just the shareholders.

In the long run, the most successful organisations are also the most moral. But what does it mean for a company to act ethically? And how can companies that claim to be ethical prove they are. Mission statements and self-enforced codes of conduct no longer cut ice. No matter what companies' stated values may be, their behaviour frequently reflects the policy that, 'if it's legal, it's ethical'.

It is often hard for managers to be ethical. There have been too many pressures to survive and to win at any cost. Proving that ethics can live with the brutal realities of global capitalism is the major challenge facing the business world.

Activities of some multinationals in the developing world have served further to tie moral concern about business activity into mainstream society.

Bad business practice, particularly in the nuclear and chemical industries, is a matter of life and death not just for current individuals, but for whole future generations. Meanwhile, the progress of European integration, with its increasingly stringent sets of standards, means that business is under increasing pressure to meet the ideals of an international culture.

Given this background, the popular argument goes, what more effective recourse could there be, than ensuring that ethical reflection and training become an established part of the management science culture?

Industry is under increasing pressure to act like a good corporate citizen – a responsible member of society. Yet which members of the organisation or society should a company be most responsible to, shareholders, employees, the environment, or consumers?

Trying to look after the interests of all such groups inevitably leads to moral dilemmas, where choices have to be made between courses of action which are all 'the right thing to do', but where leaving out any of the choices would be 'wrong'.

The central question is: when a company is faced with a moral dilemma – the need to choose between two or more mutually exclusive 'right' actions – or the need to draw up a code of ethics, who can it turn to for advice?

In Germany and the Netherlands, as well as in the US, a new profession has emerged – the ethics consultant – to provide advice on difficult moral issues. In the US, advice on ethics is increasingly available from the major accountancy and management consultancy firms.

Management consultants that employ the services of an ethics consultant are able to provide practical advice on how to deal with ethical problems. They can offer a package comprising development and implementation of codes of ethics, moral audits of a company or organisation and its direct environment, and training in analysis of ethical problems using *Dilemma Training*.

A company's code of ethics must comprise the embodiment of the company culture, rather than just bland statements about commitment to employees, consumers, and the environment. Its implementation should apply to practical issues such as when an employee's private interests should take precedence over those of the company; loyalty to the company and behaviour towards colleagues who are disloyal; an acceptable level of customer entertainment and gifts.

A moral audit surveys ethical behaviour inside and outside the company, and assesses the risks of unethical behaviour within an organisation. Are codes of ethical behaviour being maintained by employees in their contacts outside the company with suppliers and customers? Do employees and management display integrity in their dealings with others?

The US, where legislative moves have created heavy demand from corporations for advice on ethical matters, has led the way in bringing ethics services into the mainstream of consulting services.

Today's American business graduates are likely to have completed at least one ethics course, altering their perception of how ethics interact with commercial activities.

Introduction in the US over recent years of a number of statutes imposing requirements for ethical behaviour by corporations – such as the Federal Sentencing Guidelines for Organisational Crime, and the Foreign Corrupt Practice Act – have been the driving force behind the development of a market for ethics consultancy.

The sentencing guidelines, which mean that companies charged with criminal offences can see their fines significantly increased if they do not have an effective ethics system in place, have been the most important.

Some major consultancy firms in the US form have been particularly active in the field. With a business culture heavily influenced by that of its neighbour, Canada too is now seeing the rapid development of an ethics-consulting sector.

In other countries too, there is growing interest in the discipline. Although not as developed as the North American market, Europe is seeing a significant growth of interest in ethics consulting. European companies are increasingly concerned to ensure that their customers, shareholders and other groups are not plunged into a crisis of confidence because of adverse publicity about their business practices.

In any organisation, a good business ethics process is the first and most important line of defence against unethical or illegal activities. Stated simply, controls and auditing efforts are much less effective when the ethics and integrity of the organisation and its management cannot be affirmed.

Good managers are sensitive to the costs associated with a poor ethical climate. By any measure, loss of confidence in the organisation is the single greatest cost of unethical behaviour. Some of the cost drivers are: deterioration of relationships, often resulting in a damaged business reputation; declining employee productivity due to self-protective behaviour; displaced employee creativity; ineffective information flows throughout the organisation; declining employee loyalty, high employee turnover and absenteeism, and internal theft and embezzlement.

*Dilemma Training* emphasises the need for identification of stakeholders and establishment of ongoing dialogue with them. The language and intention of dialogue is very different from that of conventional consultation. Where consultation is often a passive one-way mode of communication, dialogue is an active, multi-way process. The intention is to bring the values of all parties to the table, raising issues that are important to all, and, over time, developing a higher level of understanding between participants. Whilst the information raised during the dialogue is of great importance, the development of trust and shared understanding over time is one of the key outcomes of a dialogue process.

Such dialogue can establish what values an organisation's stakeholders want to see embodied in the organisation, and how these can be translated into practice, as well as the activities and behaviour that should be promoted so that an organisation's practice is in reasonable harmony with stakeholder values.

In today's complex, global, and rapidly changing environment, it is no longer sufficient to have good thinkers at the top. The role of leadership has changed from that of the person with the right answers to that of the person with the right questions. Managers need not only develop their own critical thinking abilities, but also those of employees.

Questioning, as opposed to simply answering, allows employees to come up with their own answers instead of being provided ready-made solutions. They are thinking for themselves. The industry leaders of the future will be those who have developed critical thinkers at all levels of their organisations.

Just how do top managers acquire such skills? The most effective method is through good quality ethics training and effective support.

The point, say the consultants, is for managers to learn what they really believe and reach consensus, not by shouting or pulling rank, but by steadily and rigorously thinking the issue through together. Only in this way can they achieve lasting agreement.

Ethics consultants are better placed to facilitate such dialogues, not only because of their training and experience, but also on the grounds that it is easier for an outsider to do than it is for an insider.

**The bottom line**

It is an established fact that market leaders hold on to their position by anticipating market, social, and especially legislative changes – 'staying ahead of the game'.

**Those companies that act proactively on an ethics policy, gain immensely in terms that positively impact the bottom line – reducing exposure to legal violations, enhancing employee loyalty, satisfying pressure groups, and – most of all – convincing consumers that they are buying from people whose basic moral values are upheld even in the cutthroat environment of free markets.**

# 15

# TRAINING THE ARMED FORCES
## ETHICS IN COMBAT

---

*'That day in My Lai, I was personally responsible for killing about 25 people. Personally. Men, women. From shooting them, to cutting their throats, scalping them, to... cutting off their hands and cutting out their tongue. I did it.'*

*'When you are in an infantry company, in an isolated environment like this, the rules of that company are foremost. They're the things that really count. The laws back home don't make any difference. What people think of you back home don't matter. What matters is what people here and now think about what you're doing. What matters is how the people around you are going to see you. Killing a bunch of civilians in this way – babies, women, old men, people who were unarmed, helpless – was wrong. Every American would know that. And yet this company sitting out here isolated in this one place didn't see it that way. I'm sure they didn't. This group of people was all that mattered. It was the whole world. What they thought was right was right. And what they thought was wrong was wrong. The definitions for things were turned around. Courage was seen as stupidity. Cowardice was cunning and wariness, and cruelty and brutality were seen sometimes as heroic. That's what it eventually turned into.'*

*Soldiers from Charlie Company, after the My Lai massacre in Vietnam, 16 March 1968.*

---

The real test of the effectiveness of any ethical decision-making programme is its application in extreme situations. Apart from places like Auschwitz, it is difficult to imagine more extreme situations than those encountered by the military. This has been particularly true during the dissolution of Yugoslavia, the Gulf Wars and now the occupation of Iraq, where combat is followed by 'peacekeeping'.

It's not certain that SS guards in Auschwitz or American interrogators in Iraq's Abu Ghraib prison were necessarily conscious of doing something wrong. They probably believed that their ill-treatment of civilians was perfectly justified in the circumstances – that the ends justified the means.

Also, they were doing as they were told – obeying orders, sticking to the rules. The American interrogators possibly acted in the belief that they could get information that would save lives – American lives.

Is there anything wrong with that? If so, what?

One thing that was wrong is that it didn't take account of the *rights* of other people. But, an American soldier at My Lai, Vietnam, described women and children as 'the enemy, not people'. But if you accept that 'the enemy' *are* people, what are you supposed to do when their rights conflict with yours?

Ethical dilemmas in military operations – peacekeeping, wars and 'the war on terror' – often arise when a soldier has to choose between obeying orders and doing what he or she believes is the right course of action. However, there have been examples where soldiers have chosen to exceed their orders, and have embarked on a course of action that was plainly evil. Aside from recent cases in US interrogation centres across the world, one extreme case took place at My Lai, Vietnam, in 1968.

The soldiers of Charlie Company in My Lai couldn't claim

they were 'only acting under orders'. They were told to kill, but instead they raped, tortured and mutilated men, women, children and babies. To claim that babies are 'the enemy' reflects a complete moral and perhaps mental disintegration.

One important question is whether it was possible for any members of Charlie Company to refuse to participate in the massacre. Could any of them have actively tried to prevent it? If so, how far should they have gone? Could there have been justification for American soldiers to shoot their fellow soldiers to save Vietnamese lives?

As this book went to press, there were reports of American soldiers killing women and children in Iraq in frenzied behaviour that seemed reminiscent of My Lai.

The soldiers went on the rampage to avenge the death of a member of their unit in a bomb attack. They allegedly rounded up civilians in their houses and shot them. At least three other cases of alleged misconduct were being investigated.

In the scramble to come up with solutions, the US military promised troops in Iraq a month's crash course in 'core warrior values'. The US media reported that the course, to be conducted by unit leaders, consisted of a series of powerpoint slides dealing with principles of ethical conduct, including humane treatment of captives and wounded enemies, sanctity of the dead, and respect for personal property.

In addition, emphasis was placed on broader issues, such as the need to maintain value systems while operating abroad; and to carry out a duty to protect the weak and unarmed. In addition, various ethics-related scenarios were discussed, with trainees considering how they would react in various operational circumstances.

While some armed forces, such as the Dutch, are trying to widen the ethical compass of their members, the armies of some of the world's mightiest military powers still brainwash their soldiers into strictly following orders – shrinking their moral compass. This is easy when they are so young. They are then given deadly weapons, sent to countries and cultures entirely alien to them, deprived of home comforts and sleep, and put under enormous stress. It's not surprising that in those circumstances, torn between their conscience and their loyalty to their fellow soldiers and officers, they snap.

Members of a group, particularly a military one, are more likely to follow the decisions of the group. (This comes out in the quote at the start of this chapter.) Ethics in war are turned upside down, where a soldier's *raison d'être* is usually to kill the enemy. If he refuses to follow orders, military action is undermined and he faces a court martial. However, he can be put in situations where obeying orders means ignoring his conscience, for example, where this means the torture and murder of civilians and prisoners of war. Should he disobey? If so, why and how?

How can ethics training be an effective instrument to make such decisions in theatres of war? One possible answer is that the training 'feeds' the conscience – that the external dialogue in group training translates into an inner dialogue, an inner voice.

## The Geneva Conventions

*Guantánamo Bay has become a symbol of injustice and abuse in the US administration's 'war on terror'. It must be closed down.*

*Amnesty International, London.*

Chapter 4 explains how reference to authorities can be an excuse for not thinking for yourself – for not taking personal responsibility for your actions. In a military context, you can decide how to treat prisoners of war and civilians by referring to an authority – the Geneva Conventions. Or, if you are powerful enough, you can ignore them.

US-led troops in Iraq and Afghanistan have ignored the terms of the two conventions regarding treatment of prisoners and civilians. Prisoners have been held without fair trial, humiliated, and subjected to forbidden interrogation techniques. Civilians have been killed and wounded as 'collateral damage'; many have been rounded up as 'terror suspects' and ill-treated or killed; some have been murdered by troops on the rampage.

Was ignoring the terms of the conventions a matter of thinking *for* themselves, thinking only *about* themselves, or not thinking at all? The institutionalised breach of the conventions epitomised by Guantánamo Bay amounts to 'thinking only *about* themselves' – considering only the possible advantages to Americans and their allies, rather than attending to the principles involved. Murder of civilians in revenge killings is the result of not thinking at all.

The Geneva Conventions and their protocols are regulated by the International Committee for the Red Cross based in Geneva. As a neutral and independent body the Red Cross aims to ensure humanitarian protection during armed conflicts by exerting its right to visit prisoners of war.

The Geneva Conventions prohibit violence against prisoners, including mutilation, cruel treatment and torture, and 'outrages upon personal dignity', including humiliating and degrading treatment. They also forbid sentencing or executing prisoners without a fair trial by 'a regularly constituted court'.

Many detainees in Camp Delta, at the US naval base in Cuba's Guantánamo Bay, allege they have been tortured or subjected to other cruel and degrading treatment. Three detainees have died at the camp after apparently committing suicide. Others on hunger strike have allegedly been kept alive by painful force feeding.

US troops have also used unauthorised interrogation techniques in Iraq and Afghanistan. Beatings, some resulting in deaths, have been widely reported. Some prisoners have been fed only bread and water for up to 17 days. Others have been locked up for up to a week in cells so small that they could neither stand nor lie down. Others were soaked with cold water and then interrogated in air-conditioned rooms or in cold weather.

The US has also admitted the existence of secret detention centres outside the US, where the Central Intelligence

Agency (CIA) uses 'alternative techniques' to interrogate terror suspects. Human rights organisations such as Amnesty International pointed to the possibility of the CIA using practices which are deemed as torture under the conventions.

It took a US Supreme Court declaration to persuade the Bush administration to concede that detainees at Guantánamo Bay and other US military prisons around the world are entitled to protection under the Geneva Conventions. The US had previously claimed that certain prisoners taken in the 'war on terrorism' did not qualify for protection under the conventions.

**Example, Example, Example**

Chapter 10 referred to Gladstone's famous quote, 'Education, education, education'. Another E-word, 'Example', is equally important. To lead by example, teach by example, and change people's ways by example. If the reason for invading Iraq was to liberate its people from tyranny – as the invaders claimed – then a huge opportunity has been missed. This was the opportunity to seize the moral high ground by setting an example of how people should behave towards each other – not just under the terms of the Geneva Conventions, but according to certain moral standards.

This is where *Dilemma Training* has such a crucial role to play, a fact recognised by the Dutch military.

The Dutch military ethics handbook, *Praktijkboek Militaire Ethiek*, cites a case where soldiers 'set a good example' in circumstances that would have driven many to surrender any consideration of the ethics of their actions. The place was Srebrenica in the former Yugoslavia (see below). A 20-year-old Dutch soldier describes his experience of how he coped with his duty to protect Muslim refugees in the town, after some of the same people he was protecting had shot and killed his best friend.

The young soldier didn't react with blind rage and organise a massacre of innocent civilians. 'At first we too wanted to take revenge for what had been done to us. But you have to give a good example,' he explained.

The authors of the ethics handbook point to the fact that this young soldier, drawing on his appreciation of the need to put into perspective the desire for revenge, was able to set an example by maintaining moral standards. Such examples of restraint help to underscore the legitimacy of a peace-keeping mission.

However, despite their best efforts, the Dutch were unable to protect the town's civilians and refugees for long.

**Life after Srebrenica**

The Srebrenica massacre, Europe's worst atrocity since World War Two, was the catalyst that fired the determination of the Dutch military to improve its ethics training.

In mid-1995, two years after being designated a United Nations Safe Area, around 7,000 Muslim refugees were slaughtered by Serbian forces who overran the Bosnian town of Srebrenica, despite Dutch troops being assigned to protect the town's residents and refugees.

An enquiry reported that the Dutch peacekeepers who handed over the Muslim refugees to the Serbs were well aware of their impending fate, and that they had sacrificed the refugees for the return of about 30 Dutch soldiers kidnapped by the Serbs. Defending his decision, the Dutch commander pointed out that his forces were so inadequately equipped, and NATO air support so unreliable, that the town would have been overrun with or without the Dutch. It therefore made sense to save his own men. The report prompted the mass resignation of the Labour cabinet in The Hague.

A further incident in the same conflict, the refusal of an order by two non-commissioned officers of the Dutch signal battalion in Sarajevo, demonstrated to army personnel the importance of ethics training in operational circumstances. Both NCOs had been ordered to join a Ukrainian UN unit in the Tito barracks in Sarajevo. Because these barracks had come under fire they decided, together with their major, not to enter them.

They had been ordered not to take unnecessary risks. To keep communications open, the Signal corps tries to avoid direct combat. Therefore they chose an alternative location. However, a thousand miles away back in The Hague, a Brigadier General ordered them to enter the Tito barracks. The NCOs refused, were immediately flown back to the Netherlands, court-martialled, given a four-months prison sentence and dismissed without income.

Many were appalled by the apparent injustice. And ethical consciousness was raised by yet another notch.

It had become clear that people at all levels, from politicians to military commanders to soldiers, are confronted by ethical dilemmas before and during operations, and must be taught how to deal with them. Srebrenica put the spotlight on the urgent need for a different kind of ethical preparation for military operations.

The Dutch armed forces tackled the problem head-on. In 1999, Dutch Defence Minister, Frank de Grave, called for the establishment of the Ethics and Military Bureau at the Netherlands Defence College in Rijswijk, which developed a programme of *Dilemma Training* that could be taught to all ranks. It was dubbed the 'Ethical Decision Making Model (EDM)'.

## An Ethical Decision Making Model

*You are a tank commander and under fire from a sniper on the roof of a large building. You see the sniper. At the very moment you want to give the order to fire at the roof of the building, you see women and children on the top floor behind the windows. What are you going to do and why? Use the Ethical Decision Making Model.*

*Praktijkboek Militaire Ethiek, Dr Th A van Baarda, Prof Dr A H M van Iersel, Dr Desirée Verweij.*

The Dutch military's Ethical Decision Making Model (EDM) was developed to help make careful and balanced decisions when confronted with dilemmas. The model offers a conceptual framework, which allows people on an individual basis or in consultation with others, to arrive at an informed decision where it is difficult to decide.

By using this model against a backdrop of training and exercise situations, people learn to deal with ethical dilemmas in a more conscious manner. Moreover, if required, the model enables them to account after the event for the particular decision, both to themselves and to others.

A court martial considers only legal arguments, and not the way a soldier justifies his behaviour. It is possible to have acted legally, but to have behaved unethically. If you have acted ethically, but in breach of orders, should you have to face a court martial?

The government is ultimately responsible for the actions of its armed forces. Politicians have the ethical and legal duty to ensure that military missions are legal. If they are not legal there is little to distinguish a soldier from a violent criminal.

Aside from government responsibility, how far down the chain of military command does responsibility for ethical behaviour lie? – with officers, non-commissioned officers or the private soldier?

In November 1999, at an international conference on ethics at Britain's military academy in Sandhurst, a senior officer defined responsibility as 'affirmative action, unsupervised and without reference to a commander.'

This implies that responsibility is to be *taken* – not *given* – at crucial moments. This is especially relevant in situations where no commander is available to instruct or motivate officers or to confront them with the limits of their duties.

This means that officers are accountable to themselves for their decisions. When questioned about their choices of action, they can no longer reply 'I was only obeying orders'. It makes it absolutely essential that they are trained in taking responsibility and in justifying moral choices. At the core of military ethics lies the capacity to assess indirect effects in a split second.

The Dutch military distinguishes between three types of 'dilemma':

• moral uncertainty (not knowing how to act)

• choices between two or more conflicting right courses of action

The second category affects professions within the military, such as doctors and psychologists. They each have their own professional code of conduct which is not always compatible with that of the military, for example sanctity of life vs being part of an organisation that kills.

• choices between courses of action that all have adverse indirect (unintentional) effects.

The Dutch armed forces are part of a society that has changed

profoundly in the past few decades. Changes include secu-
larisation, individualisation, and multiculturalism. The
armed forces try to function along civilian lines wherever
possible, and the strictly military approach is adopted only
when essential to effectiveness.

According to ethics consultant, Dr Desirée Verweij, at the
Royal Military Academy in the Netherlands, these changes
in social values, for example towards human rights, are of
little practical help to the individual soldier in an operational setting, let alone when confronted with a new ethical
dilemma.

In response to this, the military is faced with either developing its own ethical standards as a kind of normative profes-
sionalism and imposing them on its personnel, or stimulating and supporting the personal responsibility of soldiers.

'The first option runs the unacceptable risk of developing a
'*Kadaver Disziplin*' in which blind obedience overrides ethical values,' says Desirée Verweij.

On the other hand, in the second option, how can individual conscience – which should be followed at all times and
under all circumstances – be prevented from having an an-
archistic effect within the organisation, where a collective
approach and group cohesion are essential?

This is the role for models of ethical decision making.

Dutch armed forces have invested heavily in ethics training.
This also involves considering recruits' potential for moral
development. Recruiting them first and subsequently training them to compensate for any deficiencies carries the risk
of their reverting to poor moral behaviour in an operational
crisis.

Recruitment takes account of some positive characteristics,
such as a democratic attitude, absence of right-wing extrem-

ism, respect for women and people of different cultural backgrounds, and not being gung-ho and trigger-happy, but displaying a professional attitude. Recruitment, selection, and education are supported by styles of leadership that act as a role model for ethical behaviour.

The training teaches how to cope with the rights and wishes of stakeholders in a dilemma. Handling ethical dilemmas in the military is not just about 'what should I do?', it is also about giving an account: 'why are you doing this?', or 'why aren't you doing that?' For example, the local population in a crisis area should be considered a stakeholder by peacekeeping forces. From this point of view, the training prepares soldiers to take responsibility on their own initiative in unforeseen situations as well as to publicly justify those choices.

**Dilemmas in combat**

The following example of a dilemma in combat is taken from the Dutch manual, *Praktijkboek Militaire Ethiek (The Practical Guide to Military Ethics)* by Dr Th A van Baarda, Prof Dr A H M van Iersel and Dr Desirée Verweij.

You are commander of an infantry unit in a war zone. Apart from regular enemy troops, there are guerrilla groups operating in the area. You receive a message from your own commanding officer that his unit has been caught in an ambush on a nearby hill. Two of his soldiers are seriously injured and in need of urgent medical help.

You make your way towards the hill to find the surrounding area strewn with antipersonnel mines. This makes it practically impossible to get to the wounded soldiers. Then one of your own soldiers appears with a man who tells you via your interpreter that he is a local farmer who lives close to the hill. You recognise him as someone you have seen through your binoculars on the way to the hill. You're convinced that he knows exactly where the mines are.

Again through your interpreter, you tell the farmer to point out a safe way to reach your commander's unit. The farmer refuses. You grab your knife and hold it to his neck. You make it quite clear that if he continues to refuse, you'll cut his throat. You are well aware that you are breaking the rules of the fourth Geneva Convention. Can you justify your action?

The situation changes. The farmer turns out to be an enemy soldier. Now you are absolutely certain that he knows exactly where the mines are. He still refuses to help. Should you use physical force to persuade him? Perhaps you should let him walk a few yards in front of you? Time is critical, and the soldiers on the hill will die if you don't act quickly.

The situation changes again. You now have radio contact with the commander of the ambushed unit. You tell him that you've captured an enemy soldier. He then orders you to force this soldier to lead you through the minefield. Should you carry out your commander's order?

**Philosophy of military ethics**

Education and training play an important role in moral development. However, a course in ethics is no guarantee of moral behaviour at the sharp end.

The Dutch military uses Aristotle's term 'moral fitness', referring to constant moral alertness. Being morally fit is the only guarantee that when confronted with moral dilemmas you will make the right decision. Moral fitness describes the degree to which you can cope with ethical issues and dilemmas under pressure.

Moral fitness – like physical fitness – requires regular training to stay in shape. It demands continuous reflection on your values, as well as reflection on what to do, and how and why it should be done. Once you are in good shape you have to make sure you stay that way.

You also need ways to measure your moral fitness. As with physical fitness, moral fitness is a process. There is no end point. It involves continuous effort to improve on past performance. For this reason moral fitness requires dialogue and debate, openness and transparency, integrity, and a willingness to correct yourself.

According to Desirée Verweij at the Royal Military Academy, the concept of 'moral fitness' implies what Aristotle called *'phronesis'* meaning 'practical wisdom'. This enables you to make the right choice – a choice based on a middle way between two extremes – for example between the use of too much force and too little. It's a matter of getting it just right.

The ability to get it right every time is acquired by habit. Aristotle states in his *Nicomachean Ethics* that '... moral virtue comes about as a result of habit, whence also its name (*ethike*) is one that is formed by a slight variation from the word *'ethos'* (habit).'

One of Aristotle's examples is 'courage', being the right middle way between fear and recklessness. Exercise of every virtue is a matter of finding the happy medium that is also right for the person concerned.

**'Moral fitness for the military must be grounded in accountability and responsibility, which are twin pillars upholding the functioning of the military in a free and democratic society,' concludes Desirée Verweij.**

# 16

# MEDIA ETHICS

*'The media are the most important means to raise ethical awareness.'*

*Robert Beckett, Institute of Communication Ethics, London.*

While on the other side of the planet media mogul Rupert Murdoch decides who'll govern Britain next, the issue of media ethics, in the wake of the Hatton enquiry into the death of weapons expert, David Kelly, has moved firmly to the forefront of public consciousness. The tables have turned – it is now journalists and broadcasters who are under public scrutiny.

The media face their own growing ethical dilemmas, which pose highly complex problems with no simple solutions. In their professional life, journalists consistently confront ethical dilemmas.

Many ethical dilemmas are specific to news gathering and reporting, such as pressure for political correctness, over-simplification of complex issues, and conflicts of interest between readers and advertisers. More recently, these extend to manipulation of images, such as alteration of pictures and reconstructions.

News gathering and writing constantly involves selection of what to include and what to leave out, how to present it and from what angle, who to quote and how to please management. Journalists make value judgements every time they start work on a story.

Basic issues include the public interest, free speech, privacy, the status of sources, revealing sources, objectivity in reporting, conduct of the media in wartime, chequebook journalism, and reporting *sub judice* cases. Recently salient issues include reporting on children, reporting on mental illness, reporting on refugees and asylum seekers, reporting on the vulnerable, avoiding the use of technology to mislead the public, and the separation of advertising from programme or editorial content in TV and radio.

But the areas of concern for media ethics are part of much wider issues of morality in communications. This is where a relatively young discipline, *Communication Ethics*, has found its niche.

### Communication Ethics – What is it?

Communication Ethics is much more than just media ethics, which is concerned mainly with news reporting, publication and broadcasting. Communication Ethics embraces media ethics, but also examines the deeper issues of how language and other forms of communication have a bearing on the way we live and our opportunities to flourish. The discipline is an answer to the problem of living '... in an age of communication without a morality of communicating' to quote ethicist Antonio Pasquali.

In a post-modern age, Communication Ethics is concerned with the ethical aspects of all human communication associated with technological and cultural changes and demographic shifts. These changes to communication contexts range from personal friendships to communication over the Internet (*netiquette*) and from classroom dialogues to mass-mediated communication in an age of diversity of race, gender, ethnicity, and cultural differences. The discipline involves an emphasis on human communication's contribution to accomplishing the desirable ends and outcomes that concern ethics in general.

Ethicist Clifford Christians in *The Ethics of Being in a Communications Context* (1997) puts Communication Ethics in Aristotelian terms by inserting *hermeneia* (language, interpretation) into the ethical decision-making process alongside *phronesis* (moral insight) and *episteme* (theoretical knowledge). According to Christians: 'In making a moral decision *hermeneia* discerns the appropriate action, in the right amount, and with proper timing. Human bonds are not constituted by reason or action but through finding common meaning in *hermeneia*'.

The Internet connects nearly one billion people in the world's first globalised electronic community. Unbounded by traditional limitations of time and space, the electronic era affects most aspects of our lives.

## Media giant tries ethics training

In May 2004 British television broadcaster, Channel 4, caved in to police pressure to drop plans to screen a documentary which claimed that Asian men in Bradford were grooming white girls for sex. The programme, which followed two mothers as they tried to track down the men who controlled their daughters by getting them hooked on drugs, claimed that some of the girls were as young as 11.

Anti-racist campaigners said the programme, *Edge of the*

*City*, would be used by far-right extremists in the run-up to local elections. The right-wing British National Party (BNP) had actively encouraged its supporters to watch the programme.

This dilemma – to screen or not to screen – was subsequently used as the case for a *Dilemma Training* session at a conference of journalists and broadcasters in Lincoln.

At least one international media organisation has put journalists through a *Dilemma Training* programme carried out by an American ethics consultancy.

The move was aimed at sharpening awareness of ethical issues faced by the media, and how to resolve dilemmas such as the need to break news first vs the requirement to respect news embargoes, loyalty to news sources vs the need to obey the law, payment of news sources vs credibility, and so on.

For decades the US government has beamed anti-Castro TV propaganda into Cuba. Several journalists on Florida newspapers have been accused of moonlighting to work on these propaganda programmes, and of taking substantial payments of government money. This was viewed as a conflict of interest and as unethical, because it seriously undermined the credibility of the journalists' coverage of US policy towards Cuba. Several have been fired.

As in the case of the US military's response to the Iraq massacres (see chapter 15), the ethics training in media organisations seems to have been reactive – bolt-on attempts to prevent reoccurrences. Yet it could have the reverse effect. Ethics training encourages people to think for themselves – to ask themselves 'is what I am doing ethically correct?' – *not* 'will what I am doing please the boss?'

It is quite possible that after such training, journalists would feel even more justified in acting in the same way, strengthened by the knowledge that what they did was ethically justifiable. Furthermore, if they are better able clearly and systematically to justify their actions after the event, they are more likely to keep their jobs.

**Media Ethical Issues**

Britain's National Union of Journalists, and the International Federation of Journalists sum up the values relevant to the media as democracy, truth, objectivity, honesty, respect for privacy, reciprocity, and responsibility.

*They describe public interest as including:*

- Freedom of expression

- Detecting or exposing crime or a serious misdemeanour

- Protecting public health and safety

- Preventing the public from being misled by some statement or action of an individual or organisation

- Exposing misuse of public funds or other forms of corruption by public bodies

- Revealing potential conflicts of interest by those in positions of power and influence

- Exposing corporate greed

- Exposing hypocritical behaviour by those holding high office

*Revealing sources and documents*
Although, in Britain, the Contempt of Court Act protects journalists from disclosure, the courts are reluctant to offer real and meaningful protection. As non-combatants,

journalists are entitled to limited protections under international law, but as witnesses to crimes of war or violations of human rights their physical safety would be greatly threatened if it becomes the practice to subpoena journalists to give testimony on what they see in the course of their work. The capacity of journalists to work without interference would be greatly reduced if the practice of obliging them to give evidence in court becomes established practice.

*Chequebook journalism*
This includes the practice of newspapers paying large sums to witnesses in criminal proceedings. The practice interferes with justice and the right to a fair trial. Bribing of witnesses to tell a particular story under oath would be unethical and a serious offence; newspaper payments sometimes come close to doing this.

*Sub judice*
The interests of justice legitimately require some restrictions on press freedom, most obviously through outlawing the publication of prejudicial material before or during a trial.

*Reporting on children*
The stereotypical images of children deployed by the media – cute baby pictures, brave children who have fought to overcome serious illness or injury, and prodigies in a variety of fields of endeavour – are not treated as individuals with lives and issues of their own. In cases involving children, journalists must demonstrate an exceptional public interest to override the normally paramount interests of the child.

*Reporting on mental illness*
There is still a wall of stigma, silence, and fear surrounding mental illness, which balanced and informed reporting can help to break down and normalise by:

- Focusing on the person being reported about, not the disability.

- Trying to present positive stories

- Trying to remove the stigma that is still attached to disabilities.

Reporters should be less judgemental about people who suffer from mental illnesses and when reporting suicides. Reporters should always be aware that when an unusual method is used by a person who has taken their own life, there is a real risk of 'copycat suicides'. They should put over the fact that people suffering from a mental health illness are not intellectually inferior to others.

*Reporting on refugees and asylum seekers*
When referring to asylum seekers or refugees, the British tabloids prefer to use negatively loaded language such as 'illegal immigrants', 'bogus' asylum seekers, 'beggars', 'scroungers', even though it is known that the use of these words or phrases is misleading, racist, and offensive. The effect of negative coverage is hostility towards refugees and asylum seekers. Verbal and physical attacks are common.

Journalists are advised to:

- seek out the views of asylum seekers and refugees.

- find out the real stories of how asylum seekers arrived in this country and investigate concerns about their treatment rather than go for negative descriptions.

*Reporting on the vulnerable*
Journalists should challenge politicians and others who seek to spread negative images of vulnerable people rather than simply recycle such views as stories.

Care is needed when using old TV footage or photographs of tragic events. This can have a serious impact on people caught up in such incidents as well as their families.

*Misleading the public*
There is a growing trend of BBC and commercial local radio stations to present as 'live' pre-recorded hourly news bulletins. Such bulletins are clearly fraudulent.

*Media freedom*
The existence of fair, free, and independent media is essential to democracy. The state must ensure that a constitutional and legislative environment exists to facilitate freedom of expression and free media. Media organisations must continue to provide the resources necessary for investigative journalism. Media workers should resolve to resist any attempts at intimidation in whatever form and from whatever quarter.

**The trade unions, NUJ and IFJ stress that governments need to strengthen existing legislation on monopolies and mergers to counter the trend towards monopolisation of provincial newspapers and regional TV companies by the few multi-national corporations.**

# PART III – BIG ISSUES

Most of the following chapters might leave you with the sense that there is nothing new under the sun. Big issues such as the rightness or wrongness of capital punishment, self-killing, mercy killing, treatment of animals and so on – issues that seem so current, immediate and so pressing – have been debated for centuries. This does not undermine their importance, but puts them in an historical context which should help avoid panic or knee-jerk reactions to them when current events bring them to the surface.

The 'big issues' chosen here are just a few among many that involve the sort of ethical choices that would benefit from the *Dilemma Training* six-step tool, where the choices involve people and non-human stakeholders occupying different positions on various eccentric circles of stakeholders.

The big issues below start with the widest circle of stakeholders, the 'environment', then to the smaller circle, 'animals', then 'other people' through examination of issues surrounding racial differences, a look at the choice of 'man vs machine' in the workplace, and – closer to home – the question of 'punishment'. This is followed by the circle of friends and family through 'euthanasia', and then at the centre – *you*. These last chapters aim to acquaint you with the sort of dilemmas surrounding 'suicide', 'assisted suicide' and 'self-sacrifice', followed by an attempt to examine what it means to be you, the decision maker – 'know thyself!'

# 17

# ENVIRONMENT – WHO IS RESPONSIBLE?

---

*'And God said unto them, Be fruitful and multiply and replenish the earth, and subdue it: and have dominion over the fish of the sea, and over the fowl of the air, and over every living thing that moveth upon the earth.'*

*Genesis, Chapter 1, Verse 28.*

---

Our relationship with the environment raises numerous ethical issues. These usually emerge in the form of dilemmas to do with economic exploitation versus environmental protection – for example, closing a factory to stop pollution vs keeping it open for protection of jobs. They also involve questions such as 'why should a particular species be protected from extinction?' and 'should we protect wilderness?'

Ethical decision making is essential to answering such questions and to resolving such issues.

This chapter goes on to look at the choices confronted by developing countries, and how industrialised countries are conducting themselves in the developing world. It also examines the choice between large scale vs small scale economic development in relation to the environmental cost – small is beautiful vs big is better. As well as political and economic, these are *ethical* choices in which the environment is one of the stakeholders.

## What is 'the environment'?

The 'environment' can be defined as *everything non-human upon which our way of life has an influence*. This would include other people, creatures and things, as well as outer space. 'Environment' in that case refers to the 'non-human world'.

It is often assumed that 'environment' implicitly applies to the *natural* environment, though the meaning 'natural' changes constantly. By 'natural', people usually mean the opposite of 'man-made', as in a beautiful mountain view.

On the other hand, as the chemical industry is quick to point out, many man-made chemicals are found in the natural environment. It is almost a cliché in chemical industry publicity material that 'everything is chemical', thus blurring the distinction between 'natural' and 'synthetic'.

Haven't they got a point? Isn't it artificial to separate humans from their environment in the first place? After all, nothing exists by itself. Everything is interconnected. If we look through a sufficiently powerful microscope, everything looks the same – a jumble of electronic particles. To quote existentialist philosopher, Jean-Paul Sartre, 'destruction is just a rearrangement of matter'. Are there any *substantial* differences among things – differences that justify their being given different *moral* treatment?

Whatever meaning you give to the word 'environment', most people would agree that we have a duty of care towards it. What this amounts to varies between cultures and individuals.

There are several theories of moral responsibility to the environment. The first is *human-centred*. According to this view, the environment is crucial to human well-being and survival. It is thus our duty to ensure that the Earth remains environmentally hospitable for supporting human life. This view is strongly underpinned by the Christian, Jewish, and

Islamic traditions, which claim that God created the world for the benefit of humans.

Sometimes theorists of this school of thought broaden their thinking to include higher animals, and grant them moral status. It is worth noting that, for these theorists, the moral obligation is *indirect*. In their view, the non-human world, with the possible exception of higher animals, has only an *instrumental* value for humans.

The most radical approach to environmental responsibility, *ecocentrism*, maintains that the environment deserves direct moral consideration in its own right. This suggests that, in terms of rights, the environment qualifies for moral personhood, that it is deserving of a direct duty, and that it has inherent value, rather than mere instrumental value. The position is that the environment is morally equal to humans. Ecocentrist approaches include deep ecology, ecofeminism, and social ecology.

Contemporary Norwegian philosopher Arne Naess coined the term *deep ecology* in 1973. Deep ecologists are concerned with searching out the fundamental roots of environmental problems rather than just responding to their symptoms. For example, they believe it is not sufficient simply to find better ways of dumping waste; we have to find ways of reducing the amount of waste we produce in the first place. Also, they attempt to replace *ego*centric (or anthropocentric) ways of thinking with *eco*centric ways of thinking – not only at the level of words, but also of deeds.

Arne Naess urges us to realise a larger and deeper sense of self by feeling a sense of commonality with the non-human world. Care automatically flows from the awareness that all living beings are intimately connected.

Deep ecology comes under *virtue ethics* in the three distinct traditions of ethics as it is concerned with the cultivation of qualities of character (see Chapter 5).

The 1980s saw the emergence of another movement, *ecofeminism* that regards the oppression of women and nature as interconnected. Karen Warren is the key philosopher, although the movement involves many thinkers from other fields. More recently, ecofeminist theorists have extended their analyses to consider the interconnections between sexism, the domination of nature (including animals), racism, and social inequalities. Consequently, it is now better understood as a movement working against the interconnected oppressions of gender, race, age, class, and nature.

There is another, non-patronising, way of regarding the environment, and that is the Buddhist way. Buddhists do not regard humans as having any particular 'stewardship' or 'dominion' over the land and the seas. They are neighbours. And the Buddhist emphasis on compassion strongly discourages harm to any beings, including forests and wilderness.

Although they believe that humans represent a higher level of spiritual development than animals, Buddhists do not believe that this gives humans any right to exploit animals. On the contrary, humans have a duty of kindness towards animals, which are believed to have the capacity for development that could justify their rebirth as higher animals or humans.

**Basically, Buddhists regard animals as being on the same path to spiritual development as humans. And animals might even have been our friends or neighbours in our previous lives as animals or humans.**

## Environmentalism – Pandas before people?

*'Oh Lord, help me to be pure – but not just yet!'*

*Aurelius Augustinus (St Augustine), 354-430 AD, Alexandria, Egypt.*

Environmentalism is often viewed as being at the cost of economic performance – a matter of choosing between the planet and the bottom line. This isn't necessarily the case. Environmental care, such as efficient waste management, and clean production, can boost profitability and public image. But in the initial stages of economic development, it is usually the case that caring for the environment is an added financial burden.

Not all countries can afford that burden. The world's ability to link economic growth to care for the global environment will depend in very large measure on whether or not the developing countries come on board.

From the developing world perspective, pressures from the industrialised nations to clean up and protect the environment seem to attach more importance to the future of the planet than to the immediate needs of the people living on it – to be putting pandas before people.

It's easy for the affluent, industrialised countries to criticise developing world environmental short-termism. 'Long-term' is devoid of any real meaning compared with the urgent business of feeding mouths. The John Maynard Keynes' quip that, 'In the long run we are all dead,' was never more appropriate.

Environmentally sustainable development is perceived as slower – more long-term – than just plain economic development – a simple logic that seems inescapable when it comes to making painful environmental decisions in the developing world.

A survey of developing world environmental legislation reveals a number of important issues, most of which involve possible double standards and ethical dilemmas. First, there is the question of the safety, health, and environmental performance of multinationals operating in developing countries. Then there is the question of a competitive advantage for local companies in countries where environmental compliance might be relatively cheap. There is also the issue of whether products such as chemicals banned in the West should be exported to countries that have not banned them.

In some developing countries there is no environmental legislation. Regulation is limited to that covered by international agreements, or required by the monetary agencies such as the World Bank. Yet, surprisingly, other developing countries, and especially the newly industrialised ones, do have a relatively complex regulatory framework. India, for example, has a labyrinth of environmental law that is more complicated than anything Europe has to offer.

There is just one major flaw – it is rarely enforced. Governments are afraid to crack down on polluters for fear of hurting already fragile economies. Polluters are usually large industries, with plenty of political muscle. Newly established environment agencies, and even ministries, are typically underfinanced and poorly staffed. What hope is there?

There is a feeling among the Organisation for Economic Cooperation and Development (OECD) countries that the developing world does enjoy a competitive advantage by virtue of having to meet weaker environmental laws than those in the West. They point to a concern that lower legislative constraints do make production costs in many less developed countries significantly cheaper than in Europe. This has even been used as an argument to resist EU proposals for tighter environmental legislation. Some major European companies have said they might consider relocating to benefit from less stringent environmental legislation.

Investigations reveal that on balance, there are few differences in corporate policy. All claim to agree that double standards are always wrong, and that environmental excellence pays off in all respects – even in savings in production costs by waste minimisation and recycling. More and more producers are adopting the same high environmental standards.

Now that most of the multinationals seem to have accepted that environmental excellence pays, they are keen to hold the high moral ground with some hard lobbying on the international circuit to get their own standards imposed on their competitors in the developing world.

Yet environmental problems seem relatively insignificant compared with finding ways out of the grinding poverty that prevails on such a huge scale in many less developed countries.

**While the industrialised world occupies itself with greening its own backyard – and looks accusingly south for sources of environmental degradation – the outlook for the developing world is still nowhere near as verdant.**

### Theoretically speaking

The rate at which the environment has shot to the top of the political agenda worldwide has left most less developed countries (LDCs) in a state of wonder – and confusion. But a sense of injustice has been quick to dawn. They point to the fact that industrialised nations have a quarter of the world's population, control 80% of its resources, and have accumulated their wealth by processes that have led to environmental destruction.

There is a sentiment that the LDCs are being pressed to do something that really belongs to a stage in their development that is still way beyond their grasp. They themselves want to be good – but not just yet. This has made them understandably defensive about environmental questions – nationalistic even. They want to develop – not be developed.

There does seem to be a moral obligation on the part of the industrialised world to compensate LDCs by giving them the aid they need to help develop in an environmentally sustainable way. The industrialised countries are often viewed as environmental missionaries preaching down from on high from where they can amply afford to be complacently sensitive about their surroundings and their health.

Only when the LDCs have reached the stage of development that most industrialised countries have already achieved do they feel that they too can give consideration to global environmental issues – when they too have the resources to do so without excessive sacrifice of their material welfare.

There is an underlying assumption that LDCs benefit from following in the footsteps of the West on environmental matters. But perhaps the present-day developing world cannot be compared to any stage in the development of the industrialised countries.

Maybe the western model is too simplistic. A number of developing world governments would probably have more sympathy with the interdependency theory, where the developing world countries, and particularly former colonies, are seen as integral to the economies of the industrialised nations. Because it supplied the industrialised world with the raw material it needed for industrialisation, the developing countries' resultant environmental problems are the industrialised world's responsibility.

**One thing must be certain – the less developed countries do have the opportunity of sidestepping the environmental mistakes of the industrialised world – an opportunity that highlights the importance of integrating environmental control in sectoral development policies, rather than cleaning up after the fact.**

## Americans abroad

There's a broad spectrum of opinion in the US about the degree of environmental consciousness with which American multinationals run their plants abroad, especially in less developed countries (LDCs). Popular rhetoric, touted by some environment groups, promotes the belief that such plants have always been operated according to lower standards than at home, and were therefore less safe for workers and the environment. An extension of this is the belief that US companies were moving operations to poorly regulated countries to escape the rising costs of compliance with ever-tightening US environmental legislation. For its part, American industry has strenuously defended its safety, health and environment record abroad.

Any complacency was exploded in 1984 by Bhopal, India, where an accident in an American-owned agrochemicals plant killed and maimed thousands of people. Bhopal gave a powerful boost to efforts to more strictly regulate working conditions in US chemical plants, and gave the chemical industry a pressing incentive to review its safety practices in LDCs, and to tighten up their control. There is now a strong consensus, from within and outside the industry, that practices in LDCs have been greatly improved, and that most foreign-owned plants usually have an environmental record vastly superior to the domestically run plants of those countries. There will, of course, always be exceptions.

However, multinationals can act irresponsibly in LDCs in other ways – for example, by continuing to market products that have been banned from home markets, or withdrawn because of a potential exposure to litigation. And there are numerous ways to cut corners. One of these is the subcontracting of hazardous manufacturing work to independent local companies. Such work may be perfectly legal, even in the US. But for these companies, avoidance of their own liability (under private law suits) is the critical issue.

The ideal course of action remains investment in cleaner production methods wherever possible, so that environmental problems are not generated in the first place.

## Is small beautiful?

*'The poor of the world cannot be helped by mass production, but only production by the masses.'*

*Mahatma Gandhi, 1931.*

When Britain started its period of industrialisation, there was little or no concern for the environmental effects. The developing countries are expected to be able to avoid the environmental mistakes of the industrialised world. Yet, if they follow the model of the industrialised nations, care for the environment in the current stage of their development could be economically premature. Industrialised nations initially accumulated their wealth at the expense of the environment.

If the industrialised world wants LDCs to industrialise in an environmentally sustainable way, there does seem to be a moral obligation for it to provide the necessary aid. This can be done by technology transfer – by giving them the know-how for clean production methods.

This is an ethical question. Decisions on how to respond to these moral claims involving allocation of resources depend on ethical decision making. In this case, the West wants the developing nations to widen their circle of stakeholders when making decisions that affect the global environment.

But there is a wider issue to deal with. It is worth challenging the assumption that developing countries will benefit from following in the footsteps of the West. For example, is large-scale industrial and agricultural production, with its associated environmental problems, essential for economic development?

Increasing the scale of production usually means moving from small-scale – handicrafts, small workshops etc. – to large-scale – more extensive organisations of production in large workplaces such as factories, and large-sized exploitation of natural resources and energy generation. Scaling up production usually makes it 'industrial'.

Industrial production processes involve complex machinery, use of diverse raw materials and complex technologies, complex technical division of labour, complex cooperation and coordination of specialised tasks, and a diverse range of skills within the workforce.

Because there is a clear limit to the level of development based on agriculture alone, due to the natural limit to demand for food, other kinds of manufacture are needed to meet needs such as clothing and housing. Whether at home or abroad, there must be industrialisation somewhere.

There is a political irresistibility to reducing dependence on imports of goods, and for provision of an industrial base to generate a military capacity for the defence of national independence.

Is this really necessary to economic development? If a country needs industrialisation to develop economically, then on what scale? Should it be large, capital-intensive, centralised production plants, or smaller, perhaps more labour-intensive, decentralised units?

Simply following in the footsteps of the developed world means large-scale industry. Not that there's any reason to assume that there is any one simple set of stages between 'backwardness' and 'modernity' common to all countries, nor one set of mechanisms for development generally.

E. F. Schumacher, author of *Small is Beautiful*, expresses the view that present-day developing countries shouldn't be compared with 19th century western nations; and that their development route must consequently be different. The differences he refers to are mainly the higher population growth of such countries, and their shortage of funds to finance capital-intensive, large-scale industries.

Large-scale industrialisation, which requires extensive capital inputs, presupposes that the country concerned is already rich. Poorer countries have to depend on foreign and multinational investment. But at a price.

The highly complex technology, design and research, involved in large-scale production remains mainly in the hands of foreign and multinational producers, who also tend to have monopoly of the organisational and technical skills for such production.

Take for example chemical fibres production. The size of initial investment, associated technology and skill requirements are beyond the means of most developing countries, and production remains firmly in the grip of huge multinational chemical concerns. This clearly undermines the 'independence' argument in favour of industrialisation.

Technical division of labour is done automatically in a chemical fibres plant. Most workers are 'operators', watching instrument panels in the plant's control room monitoring the production process. Some researchers have suggested that transfer of these kinds of jobs to the developing world is hampering development of real skills there. It is also strongly argued that the kinds of large-scale, capital-intensive technologies provide too little employment in general, either skilled or unskilled.

In more global, macro-economic terms, large-scale production can actually slow down growth in developing countries. Since it demands extensive investment this can lead to an industry's monopoly by a few huge companies. The oil industry is one example. When developing countries want their own production, the big oil multinationals are usually unwilling to invest unless they retain majority control. Preferring to maintain control through licensing agreements they rarely sell technology outright.

A primary concept used to justify large-scale plants is their 'economies of scale' – where costs per unit of production fall in relation to the size of the plant. In Brazil, large-scale production enabled high labour productivity. Economies of scale were regarded as essential to produce at prices competitive with similar scales of production in other countries.

Brazil's choice of car manufacture, for example, not only enhanced communications, but because of the large scale of its production would create important linkages – backward to indigenous rubber and steel production, and forward spin-offs such as accessories, components, new roads, petrol stations, motels etc. Not that those involved in forward linkages will necessarily thrive in harness with large industries. Small-scale workshops serving large industries can fall prey to the same exploitation as labourers.

As well as vertical integration of industrial activities, centralised industry also allows concentration of infrastructure and supporting services. But, these, together with concentration of markets and purchasing power, are usually associated with large towns, so tend to cluster around urban areas. The negative social effects of urbanisation and consequent marginalisation are well documented.

Urbanisation could be ameliorated by political moves for more equal distribution of wealth from the main towns to smaller towns, and from urban to rural areas, and to build new infrastructure around them. In practice, however, urban-oriented politicians in metropolis government rarely warm to the idea.

Many, including Schumacher, claim that decentralised, small-scale industry can more easily conform to ecological and environment demands, as well as provide job satisfaction instead of worker alienation.

Large-scale industry, whether capitalist or state-owned, needs a pool of workers selling only their labour, rather than having a share of ownership of the means of production. This, as Karl Marx suggested a century ago, alienates workers from their work, and in the initial stages of industrialisation, leads to their impoverishment. This in turn, diminishes the size of the market for goods produced, and therefore stifles economic development.

The International Labour Organisation (ILO) in Geneva – part of the United Nations – advocates decentralisation of industry to spread employment opportunities, slow down migration to urban centres, and provide more employment in small-scale manufacturing. On the other hand, the ILO says large-scale industry is perfectly acceptable if highly efficient, and with rapidly growing output. Even if direct employment is small, the indirect benefits can be considerable, it says. The industry can be taxed to fund public sector employment, and employment in other sectors can be financed from savings in imports. But, the ILO admits that these benefits rarely occur in practice, and that employment usually drops, and profits simply accrue to the capitalist owners.

Karl Marx 1818-1883

Many developing countries have chosen large-scale industrialisation under the influence of the former Soviet model.
They have identified their own situation with that of pre-in-
dustrial Russia, and have viewed the Soviet way as a means
to achieve industrialisation under state control, while avoiding the pitfalls of capitalism.

This was because the former Soviet Union, which too was
'backward' compared with Britain and other capitalist industrialised nations, was still able to develop without mort-
gaging itself to foreign countries, and without exploiting
any colonies (it had none). Its independence of foreign control allowed it to concentrate on development of producer

goods industries, rather than consumer goods. The human cost, however, is well documented.

Gandhi said the poor of the world cannot be helped by mass production, but by production by the masses. He wasn't anti-industry. He advocated small-scale manufacture; not just for economic reasons, but to support the 'whole man' concept to avoid worker alienation consequent upon industrial division of labour. With certain exceptions most theorists appear to agree that raising living standards depends on the existence of a dynamic and growing industrial sector somewhere.

Whilst there is much support for small-scale, decentralised industries, there are no examples of its success as a credible alternative in developing countries. Those western nations that have the potential to head in that direction are already highly developed, after having passed through a long period of large-scale industrialisation and urbanisation. They are now entering a post-industrial information technology age where decentralised cottage industries can be run from electronic offices in the home.

Whether, as Marx suggests, there is an historical inevitability about all this, is questionable. But potential realisation of the small-scale vision, whether viewed through populist, anarchist or communist eyes, does seem so far to be a development that springs out of industrialisation, whether capitalist or socialist.

**If there is an alternative way to reach the final goal by sidestepping the large-scale industrialisation stage, it has yet to emerge. And this is unlikely to come about in the developing countries unless they can somehow be left to progress independently of global, capitalist economic forces.**

## How green is my revolution?

As mentioned above, one way for the industrialised countries to help the developing world is by giving it the technology it needs to progress. 'Technology transfer' can be an act of generosity. But intervention of any kind should be treated with caution. Whether licensed for profit or as part of an aid package, it can have unexpected and unwelcome social consequences.

Famine in India in the 1960s, and consequent dependence on politically charged US aid, led to adoption of new agricultural technology aimed at producing high-yield varieties of wheat and rice. Known as the *Green Revolution*, it came about swiftly – with unseemly haste, some say – and with little regard for social consequences.

It was a complete technological package comprising specially developed high-yield seeds, plus an artificial environment, dependent on fertilisers, agrochemicals, and irrigation. Whilst expensive, their application enabled production of two or more crops per year instead of one. This heightened the time-bound nature of planting and harvesting, which in turn demanded greater use of organised labour inputs at crucial periods, and mechanisation to speed up operations.

The results have been an unqualified success – but only in terms of raising agricultural output, and national income. However, increased national income does not necessarily lead to improved living standards and wealth distribution. The crucial question is not how much is produced, but who gets it.

Green Revolution biochemical technologies had pretensions of neutrality to the scale of production and to suitability for small producers, but they depend on timely, mechanised irrigation. And the time constraints of multiple cropping demanded mechanisation of harvesting and other activities.

Mechanisation meant labour displacement, and larger land holdings for economies of scale. This also meant investment. Only the rich farmers could afford this. But it meant they had less liquid capital to lend to poorer farmers.

New technologies were 'knowledge intensive'. To apply them, and gain their full potential, farmers needed to be trained in their use. Class ties with officials disseminating information, greater social standing and literacy, gave rich peasants privileged access to required training.

Finally, the rich farmers' capacity to store production gave them the advantage of selling at high prices during shortages.

**Particularly at a time when developing countries are being offered genetically modified (GM) crops as part of 'green revolution' packages, this case illustrates the importance of rigorously examining every possible angle, and taking account of all possible stakeholders before making decisions as profound as those connected with intervention – philanthropic or self-serving – in the name of aid, technology transfer or any other form of 'assistance'.**

# 18

# SCIENCE – PLAYING GOD?

When American atom bombs hit Hiroshima and Nagasaki in 1945, they exploded the dreams of many scientists – dreams that nuclear physics would be harnessed to improve the planet, and the future of those living on it. The result was a post-war scientific backlash, in which many of the best brains in nuclear physics changed course to a science that had been around a lot longer than splitting atoms – biotechnology. It was also a science that was seen as benign – a view still supported by most of the scientific community. But it is a perspective that is not always shared by the public and the media. There is real concern that human beings are playing with too much power.

Their unease is understandable. Unlike nuclear explosions, release of genetically engineered organisms is not a once in time and space event. Organisms cannot be recalled. A decision to release them is irreversible – and so are the effects. Biotechnology's diversity will leave no one untouched – for better or for worse. It is not the mere introduction of a new product or process technology. It is a whole new set of techniques as potentially varied as life itself, and one which could influence most forms of life.

There is also the objection in principle, that while it is not fully understood how the genetic engineering side of biotechnology works, there is always the possibility of unpredictable, and perhaps catastrophic, results.

But the other side of this double-edged sword is the belief that biotechnology holds the key to feeding and greening the planet, without sacrificing economic growth – that science can cut a path to a Utopia where new economic activities can be generated from natural resources without depleting them in the process.

Reality, as usual, probably lies somewhere in the middle of these extremes. But as commercial pressures intensify, there is a growing feeling among environmentalists and many legislators that, whilst the initial fears of accidental release of a genetically engineered organism that 'goes wild' might have been exaggerated, there is an urgent need for tighter regulation.

**Inheriting some difficult dilemmas**

Biotechnology has been around a long time in less sophisticated forms. For millennia, yeast and other microbes have been used to leaven bread, make yoghurt and brew beer. And it was as long ago as 1885 that Louis Pasteur developed the first vaccine. But in the past two decades biotechnology has gained two powerful implements – genetic engineering and recombinant DNA technology. By controlling the genes – the biological instructions that determine the nature and appearance of a living organism – genetic engineering can create completely new life forms.

In addition to the power to completely destroy life, scientists now have the power to control even its molecular basis. They can change the world – literally. Not all would agree that changes that are now possible would necessarily change the world for the better, nor that scientists and governments are necessarily the ones who should be entrusted with deciding what would make the world a better place.

Can the democratic process – in the developed western world – maintain a grip on its developments? And what are the prospects for its use in societies where governments are not under the direct influence of the public?

Objections can be broken down into two broad categories – those concerned with the practical effects on the environment, and those that are concerned with the moral issues. Most objections are based on blends of both in various proportions.

The moral objections concern mainly inviolable principles – such as objection in principle to an 'unnatural' interference with the genetic structure of living things – the notion of 'playing God'. Another, stemming from the first, is that life forms 'created' by humans could be reduced to the status of commodities solely for the service of their 'creators'. This objection seems to have credence only within the more pragmatic context of the belief that survival of the planet depends on humans existing with and alongside other living species, rather than through the exploitation of them.

**Pressure to behave ethically**

The most basic arguments against biotechnology include moral rules such as we should not interfere with nature, and we should not alter the genetic constitution of organisms. The first is relatively easy to dispense with on the grounds that humans and what they do are part of nature; and that the survival of any species depends on its adapting nature to its needs as well as its needs to nature.

Opposition based on the belief that genetic engineering breaches the integrity of a species does not stand up because of the natural plasticity of species.

Another way of judging the rightness or wrongness of the technology is to look at the consequences of using it. Any arguments against genetically engineered micro-organisms because of their perceived environmental or health effects could be applied equally to non-genetically engineered organisms. The risks are dependent on the end-product, not on their method of production, a standpoint recognised by the US Environmental Protection Agency, whose regulations do not distinguish between genetically or non-genetically modified organisms, but which focus on the properties of organisms themselves.

The main controversy centres on intentional release of genetically engineered bacteria and the possibility that they might damage or disrupt ecosystems. This occurs mainly in agriculture. The genetic engineering of plants that have improved nutritional value, are resistant to drought, have lower dependence on nitro-fertilizers, and which in some cases reduce the environmental impact of farming, can be regarded only as good.

But the main point is that release of genetically engineered micro-organisms takes place in the context of modern farming methods, which already rely heavily on chemical pesticides. Although there is a possibility of undesirable ecological effects of biotech products, there is already the certainty that many pesticides have an undesirable environmental impact. Because biotech products replace chemical ones, this amounts to replacing a certain danger with a merely possible danger.

It has been claimed that genetic engineering, like nuclear science, confers a power on humans for which they are psychologically and morally unprepared.

This highlights the inadequacy of international controls. Just as certain regimes have developed a nuclear programme for unethical uses, there is no way of enforcing worldwide regulation of biotechnology against uses such as eugenic or military.

Aside from these complex and value-based ethical issues,

there are numerous practical objections to biotechnology. Few condemn the science outright – most express concern about the research stage and the release of new organisms into the open environment. Such fears are currently reflected in efforts to tighten regulation of biotech activities.

## Unfolding the mysteries of creation

Biotechnology is basically about speeding up evolution. The major breakthrough was the determination in the mid-1940s of the genetic building block, deoxyribonucleic acid (DNA). By 1953, biochemists Watson and Crick, had worked out what the DNA molecule looks like. It is basically made up of two chains of atoms twined round each other. There are four 'links' in the chain, called 'bases', which are the basic units of genetic information. DNA in all organisms is built around four bases.

The sort of manipulation achieved today was a pipe dream as recently as the mid 1960s. A foretaste of the powers of creation came in the 1970s, when scientists discovered that certain parts of the DNA chain control certain genetic functions, such as the number of limbs. Manipulation became possible in the early 1970s, following the discovery that certain enzymes can split the chain so that parts from the chains of other organisms can be added to it in a sort of 'cut and splice' editing process. It was this development which led to the first truly genetically engineered product, human insulin in the early 1980s, and its marketing by the mid-1980s.

Anti-cancer agent, interferon, and human growth hormones followed. Biotech scientists have since turned their attention to a number of other key areas, the most prominent of which is agriculture. Plant research has focused mainly on development of new varieties with frost resistance, improved yields and enhanced resistance to agrochemicals, and especially to herbicides. In animal research, a cross between a goat and a sheep was patented as long ago as 1987.

And the concept is a lot older than that. Genetic manipulation has been carried out by farmers, animal breeders, bakers and brewers for thousands of years – sometimes deliberately, but usually by accident. The mule, for example, a hybrid between the horse and the donkey, has served as a useful, genetically engineered tractor for thousands of years. Plant husbandry has traditionally involved development of new strains. The difference with application of biotechnology is that developments that would otherwise take several growing seasons to achieve, can be done in a laboratory in as many weeks. It is genetic engineering and DNA manipulation that now form the main components of biotechnology.

## Mutants on the march?

The public trust in scientists vanished with Chernobyl and Bhopal. Although many of the scientists involved in pioneering biotechnology had left the nuclear industry because of unease about the direction it had taken, environmentalists have drawn uncomfortable comparisons between the two industries. Not only are the industries similar in the way they attracted the best in scientific brainpower and the investment interest of major corporations, they also produced some unexpected public fears about what happens if mistakes are made. In the case of biotechnology, it is the effects of compounding the genetic changes in organisms which, if they escape into the open environment, could continue to multiply their mutations in an uncontrolled chain reaction which could have unpredictable results.

Fears that genetically engineered micro-organisms could break out of laboratories and escape into the environment to reproduce monsters, mutations and plagues, have subsided into reservations of a more specific kind. One example is the concern that a gene to protect a crop from the effects of a particular weed-killer could leak through natural crossing of the engineered plants into weeds, producing super herbicide-resistant weed varieties.

The same fears apply to plants into which the insecticidal toxins from *Bacillus thuringiensis* have been engineered, and where biotechnology is used to develop strains of crops that are high-yielding, although highly agrochemical-dependent. There is a danger of leakage to produce high-yield, herbicide and insect-resistant weeds.

Another common objection is that the users of herbicide-resistant plants are also bound to use a particular herbicide, which could give the producer an unfair competitive position. Major pesticide producers are now the world's largest seed producers. Also, biotechnology usually involves the accelerated evolution of particular organisms. But the fact that their environment does not evolve at the same pace, could produce some unpredictable results.

**Ethicists regard the technology as a double-edged sword – with enormous potential benefits, but still open to abuse. Aside from the economic, social, and political arguments, again the decision whether or not to use this technology is an ethical one, made all the more difficult, not just because of the difficulty of taking account of the rights of all stakeholders, but especially because of the unpredictability of its environmental and social impact.**

## You're never alone with a clone

*'We simply cannot stand by and allow humans to be copied. That would be breaking through an ethical barrier that goes far beyond even the barrier of the atomic bomb.'*

*Jürgen Rüttgers, Minister for Research, Bonn, Germany, 1996.*

News of the world's first clone of an adult sheep in the mid-1990s triggered a knee-jerk negative reaction from politicians and religious leaders worldwide, and fuelled the debate on the usefulness and dangers of such experiments.

In a major breakthrough at Edinburgh's Roslin Institute a single cell from an adult ewe's udder was 'mated' with a prepared unfertilised egg and implanted into a surrogate mother. The result was the creation of the world's first adult clone, in the form of Dolly the sheep, genetically identical to the sheep from which the cell was taken. The scientists involved said the developments could be applied to human cloning soon, and that there should be international laws preventing such work.

The major concern now surrounds human cloning. Human cells subjected to controlled freezing, using special protective chemicals like those used with Dolly, could technically be cloned, bringing the image of the person – if not their personality – back to life.

But who would want human clones? It has been suggested that examples might include parents who have lost a child and want to produce an identical replacement; ego trippers of various kinds wanting to produce copies of themselves; patients with a serious illness wanting a 'twin' for spare part surgery.

Are we entering the age of asexual reproduction, virgin births of identical copies of the mother, and resurrection of genetic duplicates of the dead? How serious are these possibilities? The scientists dismiss them as fantasy. But the world's politicians are worried. Human cloning is already illegal in Britain. Moves to introduce similar legislation are underway around the world.

Ten years ago German Research Minister, Jürgen Rüttgers, called for a worldwide ban on cloning human beings and denounced pro-cloning arguments used by some scientists saying they mirrored the Nazi way of thinking. Rüttgers said it was 'perverse' to defend the possibility of cloning humans for medical reasons, such as making it easier to transplant organs. 'Humans would be then bred for spare parts and then later carved up,' he said. 'That is exactly the same thinking that drove the Nazis to their research on human breeding.'

The preoccupation with nightmare visions of human cloning has diverted attention from the enormous benefits that could derive from animal cloning in terms of food production and health care. While the cloning of a sheep whipped up fears of mad scientists making copies of Stalin and Hitler, gene therapy companies are steadily working towards cures for diseases such as cancer, cystic fibrosis, and AIDS.

The technology has the potential to offer vast benefits, such as saving endangered species, developing new treatments for haemophilia, and the production of transgenic animals to provide proteins, blood, and organs.

In conclusion, it would seem that there is little unethical about genetic engineering of micro-organisms itself, or animal cloning, but that its ethical acceptability depends on finding a way to eliminate risks of its misuse. This will depend partly on appropriate global legislation and its effective enforcement. But laws rarely anticipate problems. They tend to be reactive – introduced after the events they are designed to control. They are nearly always one step behind. Furthermore, legislators are rarely able to foresee and therefore deal with all aspects of a new technology's application. And people are amazingly clever at circumventing laws. Raising consciousness of the ethical issues involved through *Dilemma Training* can be an effective method of filling the shortcomings of legislation.

**Against the backcloth of Middle Eastern conflict, just a brief glimpse at similar efforts to control misuse of nuclear technology and chemical weapons does arouse quite some cause for concern about the possible misuse of biotechnology and human cloning. This needs to play a prominent role in the decision-making process when considering the technology's application.**

# 19

## ANIMALS – CAN THEY SUFFER?

*The day may come when the rest of the animal creation may acquire those rights which could never have been withholden from them but by the hand of tyranny. The French have already discovered that the blackness of the skin is no reason why human beings should be abandoned without redress to the caprice of a tormentor. It may one day come to be recognised that the number of the legs, the villosity of the skin, or the termination of the os sacrum, are reasons equally insufficient for abandoning a sensitive being to the same fate. What else is it that should trace the insuperable line? Is it the faculty of reason, or perhaps the faculty for discourse? But a full-grown horse or dog is beyond comparison a more rational, as well as a more conversable animal, than an infant of a day or of a week, or even a month, old. But suppose they were otherwise, what would it avail? The question is not, Can they **reason**? nor, Can they **talk**? but, Can they **suffer**?*

*Jeremy Bentham, philosopher, 'Introduction to the Principles of Morals and Legislation', 1789.*

The question of how we should treat animals poses major ethical problems. Ethical decision making needs to take account of the rights and wishes of all stakeholders. These include not only the environment, but also those non-human creatures who inhabit it.

When accounting for animals in decision making, for example, animal experimentation vs human suffering, certain questions need to be answered.

What status do animals have relative to humans. The 'burning house' thought experiment might help. Look at the sketch of the burning house on page 20, and imagine your dog and other pets at one window, and a convicted paedo-phile at the other. Which will you rescue?

Do animals have a right to life or to be free from pain? Advocates of animal rights point to the extent that animals suffer at the hands of humans. How do we know they do? But what counts as suffering? Animals do not have a human language to communicate it.

On the other hand, in animals' favour, it is easier to lie or pretend with words. When an animal screeches with pain, can we really doubt it is in pain? Humans, on the other hand, can fake pain. Can animals fake pain? And the reverse – can animals be in pain, but not show it (not even through body language)?

Does the hyena pacing up and down its cage in a zoo suf-fer? Does suffering have anything to do with depriving an animal of its usual habitat? Does a bird need space to fly, a panther to run, or an elephant to live in herds? Is it only on the basis of behaviour that we can ascribe mental states to animals – mental states such as the grief expressed through a whale's howling when her calf has been killed?

Sacrificing animals or experimenting on live animals has been an integral part of many scientific tests and observa-tions, religious rites, industrial practice, and the way many people live their lives. Government regulations require the use of animals to test the toxicity levels of drugs, cosmetics, cleaners and other industrial and household products.

Some medicines, such as the polio vaccine, depend on the sacrifice of chimpanzees. The same holds for Chinese medi-cine, for example, using rhinoceros horn as an aphrodisiac, or live snake's blood for longevity. Cows, pigs, and chickens are raised and slaughtered for food. Poor living and trans-port conditions of farm animals are increasingly questioned. How can such practices be justified?

People advocating theories about the moral status of animals fall into two main groups, similar to those mentioned above in respect of the environment: those advocating *indirect* duties, and those advocating *direct* duties towards them. Most philosophers have held that our obligations toward animals are only *indirect*, and derived from purely human interests.

Although the ancient Greek philosopher Pythagoras (c. 569-475 BC) believed animals had souls, and that it was wrong even to eat them, the views of Aristotle and his successors were more influential, and were later absorbed into Christian doctrine. For Aristotle there was obviously a hierarchy in nature with men firmly at the top!

Theologian and philosopher, Thomas Aquinas (1225-1274), and German philosopher, Immanuel Kant (1724-1804), both believed that cruelty to animals could corrupt – could lead to cruelty among human beings. They viewed kindness to animals as serving the interests of humanity rather than of the animals. Aquinas also added that, because animals are the *property* of humans, it may be wrong to harm someone else's animal.

French philosopher Nicolas Malebranche (1638-1715) claimed that all suffering is a consequence of Adam's sin and, because animals are not descended from Adam, they cannot suffer. On the other hand, it could be argued that animals are God's creatures, and therefore deserving of care.

More recent philosophers have argued that animals have a direct moral standing, and therefore should be spared pain for their own sake, and not merely for the sake of how this affects humans.

Classical utilitarianism in particular maintains that moral actions are those that promote the greatest amount of pleasure and the least amount of pain. Because animals experience pleasure and pain, their interests count directly. This is the position advocated by contemporary Australian philosopher Peter Singer.

Utilitarians regard suffering as undesirable, and so they believe it should be minimised wherever possible. If it is suffering itself that is undesirable, then there is no obvious reason why only human suffering should be taken into account. Suffering of all sentient beings should be minimised. On the other hand, utilitarianism makes it morally permissible to arbitrarily make an individual suffer for the benefit of the greater good. This could justify painful animal experimentation.

There are several counterarguments to utilitarianism. One insists that utilitarians are wrong in putting a purely negative connotation on pain. Scientists often argue that scientific knowledge is of such a high value that it can demand sacrifices – 'no pain, no gain'.

Another objection is that there is a danger of losing sight of the very real differences between animals and humans. Surely, it is claimed, the clear differences justify different treatment? This line of argument has been condemned by its opponents as 'speciesist' – like racist and sexist, but in this case arrogantly discriminating against members of a different species. 'Anti-speciesism' now constitutes a major issue in the debate about the treatment of animals.

For much of western civilisations' history, animals have been regarded as property. If animals are regarded merely as human property, they are given no intrinsic value. Animals such as dogs and cats have a special place in the hearts of humans, so they acquire an indirect moral standing. But other animals such as rats are not cared about so their moral standing is virtually nonexistent.

Philosopher Tom Regan explains that a being has inherent worth when it is a subject of a life, when it has preferences, beliefs, feelings, recollections, and expectations. Many animals exhibit these features and therefore have inherent worth. Regan criticises alternative criteria of inherent worth. To say, for example, that only intelligent – or self-conscious – beings have inherent worth, would be to exclude infants and some mentally disabled people. To claim, therefore, that only humans have inherent value is speciesist bigotry.

When Charles Darwin (1809-1882) argued that humans' affinity with the animal kingdom was a matter of scientific fact, the animals' cause seemed to get a boost from within science itself. Darwin's theory of evolution suggested that humans and animals differ only in degree, not in kind. Opponents of racism argued that such prejudices were formed by making moral distinctions on the basis of illusory differences; the idea took root that ill-treatment of animals might reflect the same kind of mistake. This set the stage for the contemporary debate on the moral status of animals and the ethics of animal experimentation.

Can humans claim a privileged position over the rest of the natural world? To some thinkers the notion of a *right*, as in 'animal rights', involves not only the ability to make a claim against someone, but also presupposes that:

- someone has *choices* (therefore a *free will*);

- is *rational*;

- has the ability to enter into reciprocal relationships.

Therefore, the argument goes, because animals do not have these attributes, they have no rights. Of course, on this basis, not only would animals have no rights, but, again, neither would infants or the people with certain mental disabilities.

The anti-speciesist argument is often advanced in terms of rights. If there are no morally relevant differences between humans and other animals, then other animals should enjoy the same rights as humans – such as the right not to be ill-treated or experimented upon. A counterargument is that rights come from the capacity to make moral choices and the need to exhibit morally responsible behaviour. However, in the animal world, there is no notion of moral responsibility, hence there is no basis for animal rights. On the other hand, some animals do exhibit seemingly moral behaviour, for example, elephants feed injured members of their species.

Talking in terms of rights can seem obscure. The idea of assigning rights to beings who can never know that they have them, so could never enforce them, even if they had the means, may seem an empty gesture. If the issue boils down to how humans ought to behave, perhaps it makes more sense to focus on the humans, rather than the animals.

French philosopher, René Descartes (1596-1650), asked how you know that animals really do feel pain? As the quest for scientific knowledge gathered pace, his theories conveniently opened the door to justification of animal experimentation. Descartes decided that animals not only did not have souls, but were nothing more than very sophisticated machines. Machines cannot feel pain, nor, therefore, can animals. Animals just behave as if they were in pain. He supported his position by citing the fact that animals do not engage in sophisticated language, which is the prime indicator of rationality.

One counterargument is that, whilst animals have no spoken language, they do have body language. Whilst spoken language can lie, body language is a truer reflection of feelings – it is as credible, if not more credible, to believe that an animal howling and writhing is in pain, than a human saying, 'I am in pain'. Also, animals are used for pain research. This would make absolutely no sense if it were believed that they did not feel pain.

Until recently, the argument was widely accepted that animal experimentation was generally justified, given its potential for relieving human suffering. However, the picture has become clouded by the increasing emphasis on prevention being better than cure – it is better to discourage humans from smoking than to force beagles to smoke in the search for a non-carcinogenic cigarette.

Anti-speciesists argue that the reason experiments are carried out on animals undermines their moral justification. The point they make is simple. The only reason experiments are performed on animals is that they are sufficiently similar to humans to make the experimentation worthwhile. If they were not, it would not be rational to draw conclusions from them that could be applied to humans. But if they are sufficiently similar to humans for this purpose then they should be treated with similar moral respect. Perhaps this case is a little too simple.

Similarity is not the same as identity, and it could still be argued that the differences that remain between humans and animals are sufficient to justify different treatment. Indeed, the argument boils down to differences of opinion over which differences between humans and animals are morally relevant, and this cannot be a straightforward matter of fact.

The idea that the basis for our treatment of animals should lie, not so much in reasoned argument, but in feelings or attitudes towards them, is found in a number of emerging 'green' philosophies. Many contain a strongly spiritual, even mystical, strain that emphasises the importance of experiencing an essential unity of the natural world, of which humans and animals are a part.

**However, the danger of such an all-encompassing view of the moral community is that all distinctions tend to blur, making it difficult, to decide, for example, which is worse – killing a human or a head louse.**

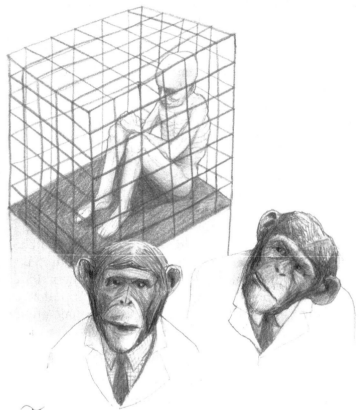

The reason we have to experiment on them
is that they are so much like us.

## Animals, pets, religion & vegetarianism

Evolutionary theories have become part and parcel of the way we currently think about the distinction between human beings and animals. The belief that the difference between humans and animals is one of *kind*, rather than *degree*, has become much more controversial. Some people now even prefer the phrase 'non-human animals' to 'animals'. Nevertheless, *The Bible* has, over a very long period of time, been immensely influential in creating the counterassumption that humans occupy a higher space than other creatures in the hierarchical order of being. Humans alone, the biblical account tells us, are created 'in the image of God' and they have been given unlimited dominion over all things, living or otherwise. There is, in other words, a God-given licence to put everything non-human at the disposal of God's people. In Genesis 1, 28, we read:

> '... be fruitful, and multiply, and replenish the earth, and subdue it, and have dominion over the fish of the sea and over the fowl of the air, and over every living thing that moveth upon the earth.'

In what way do humans differ from animals? Can humans think and reason whereas animals cannot? Do animals think about their own thinking? Do they have self-consciousness? Do animals have a language? Can they play games and laugh, like humans do? Do they have feelings like us?

In the Ancient World, at the time of the Greek philosopher, Sextus Empiricus, the rationality of animals was defended using what has become a famous example: Chrysippus' dog. When tracking a prey, the dog comes to a crossroads with three exits. After sniffing two of them and failing to pick up the scent, he chooses the third exit without trying to pick up the scent first. The dog must therefore be reasoning, it was claimed.

The behaviour of dolphins or apes challenges many of our

assumptions about animals' lack of intelligence. Dogs are often depicted in pictures of philosophers. Their tenacity and fidelity symbolise what is needed when searching for wisdom. Apes display many human characteristics, such as in playing games, appreciating and making jokes, teasing each other, communicating with others, making and using tools and being bored. (In Amsterdam zoo, when a gorilla was allowed to watch TV his behaviour became less destructive than it had been.)

These characteristics all require some degree of consciousness, but to what extent do apes have self-consciousness? How can self-consciousness be measured and why is it so important as a criterion for deciding on the moral status of these creatures and how humans should behave towards them?

To understand the differences and similarities between humans and animals, it is worth taking a look at what criteria apply to being a human.

Contemporary Canadian philosopher Charles Taylor argues against human superiority and moral privilege. In his view, humans are only different in the sense that they are shaped by language in two important ways. Firstly, their self-understanding is shaped through the linguistic concepts they use to shape their thoughts and emotions. What otherwise would remain confused or chaotic is given shape and in that sense defined, Taylor claims.

An example could possibly be the following. To call what is at any one moment a mixture of physical sensations, thoughts and feelings, 'love' is to give it a form that it wouldn't have had without that vocabulary. Not only does language define feelings, but the evaluative terms that we use also define and redefine what it means to be human. According to Taylor, we understand persons and human nature by using linguistic concepts such as 'love', 'autonomy' and 'dignity'.

Secondly, he states that we are born into a community that shares a language and a set of understandings. Clearly, animals do not use human language. A chimpanzee does not use the concept 'freedom'. This is because the meaning of the term depends on a community of language users of which it is not a member. It therefore cannot claim, or even think, that it has been deprived of its freedom when put in a cage. Its conception of freedom is either nonexistent or very different from a human conception of freedom.

A chimpanzee could have all sorts of beliefs about freedom, its cage or the people that experiment on it, but that would only be through its own stock of concepts that it shares with others of its community.

However, these differences do not justify a lack of moral duties towards animals.

Speciesism – that is, an improper lack of respect for the lives, rights, and needs of animals other than the human species – is morally wrong only if it can be shown that the differences between animals and humans are not profound.

It has been argued that being empathetic or not is profoundly relevant. If animals are not capable of treating humans as moral beings they cannot themselves be worthy of those same moral considerations. But the same could be said for babies, for people with certain kinds of mental disability or illness, and for those in a coma.

It could be argued that though such people might not be fully capable of being moral agents, they have been once, or may be one day, whereas animals never have been and never will be (unless they are part of a cycle of reincarnation).

When it comes to profound similarities, the most relevant question, to quote Jeremy Bentham again, is can they suffer?

It could be argued that if suffering is bad, if it is in our power to reduce suffering we should do so. This is the line taken by Peter Singer, whose unorthodox ethical beliefs have supported the foundation for the growth of the animal rights movement. It is a standpoint that has demanded a lot of courage. His views are met with naked aggression, suspicion and hysteria. His lectures have been sabotaged, his books banned and his courses cancelled.

He challenges us to focus on questions such as 'what constitutes a person?', rather than a human being, and 'what are the criteria for a flourishing life?' Many people fiercely object to his reduction-of-suffering argument because it often directly conflicts with the Judeo-Christian *sanctity of human life* principle, which excludes a moral duty to non-humans.

Contemporary British philosopher Roger Scruton objects to what he claims is an absence in Peter Singer's moral views of an explanation of how animals differ from humans. There is a difference of some sort and this needs to be accounted for in any moral theory, Scruton insists. Humans question what is right and wrong, whereas dogs and jellyfish don't. Humans are animals with choices, whereas (other) animals only have desires. The fact that part of our vocabulary consists of words such as 'rights', 'responsibility', and 'duty' suggests that humans are not driven purely by needs and wants, in the way that animals are.

Roger Scruton appeals to currently accepted insights in 'philosophy of mind' when he introduces the following categories: some animals have sensations only, such as jellyfish, other animals such as rabbits also have emotions and, finally, some animals also have beliefs and learning. This last step is a transition from *quantity* to *quality* – animals becoming moral beings – and this category of creatures include humans and possibly elephants, dolphins, and apes.

On the other hand, whilst inclusion in the moral community has its benefits, it also carries the huge burden of being responsible for one's actions. To regard, say, cats as moral beings would involve penalising them as mass murderers.

Scruton continues by claiming that how the various animals should be treated doesn't necessarily depend on their place in this hierarchy, but more on the kind of relationships we have with them. Of course, it is extremely difficult to state anything with any certainty about what goes on in the mind of an animal. Also, the role of language for consciousness seems to be ignored. With Wittgenstein we could argue that if lions could talk, we wouldn't understand them, that is, their language would make sense only to lions that share a similar set of concepts.

Often the concept *instinct* is used as a means of describing the difference between human behaviour and that of animals. Does the concept indeed clarify, or does it further obscure, what is an already fuzzy distinction? 'Instinct' often means innate behaviour, the kind that is outside an individual's control. Even very complex tasks can be accomplished by animals with the help of their instinct as opposed to having to reason their way through, as humans need to do. This was the belief of, for example, Aristotle and the Stoics.

However, couldn't it be argued that the need to reason is in itself an instinct, that is, it is an innate behaviour that is outside our control and necessitated by surviving specific environments? If not, in what ways are our genetically determined ways of thinking and behaving different from 'instincts'?

Perhaps it is helpful to distinguish between different kinds of animals. Some animals we need for our own survival, for example, for agriculture or food. However, machines have almost completely replaced animals as beasts of burden in agriculture, at least in the West, and it can be questioned what 'survival' means. Do we need to eat meat for survival?

Vegetarians are people who object to eating meat for one or a combination of reasons. Some vegetarians don't eat meat, because they think that it is morally wrong for us to kill animals just because we enjoy eating their meat; and that many animals are kept, raised, and killed cruelly. For example, they are not given enough space or light; they are kept in unnatural conditions which cause abnormal behaviour; or they endure painful slaughter.

People who have chosen to become vegetarian on the basis only of the second of these reasons could still eat the meat, for example, of a pheasant that they had accidentally driven over with their car, or of a sheep that was painlessly killed after it had experienced a long and happy life in the meadow.

However, whereas people who were vegetarian for the first of these reasons could eat the pheasant, they could consume the sheep only if it were made clear that the animal was not killed specifically for its meat, but rather for, say, compassionate reasons and that its slaughter shortened its suffering.

Another objection is that animals can suffer and feel pain, and it is wrong to cause unnecessary pain. But what evidence do we have for the claim that animals with primitive nervous systems, such as prawns or snails, can feel pain? Also, if the suffering of animals is eliminated or at least minimised – as in organic husbandry – is it then still justifiable for humans to eat their meat?

A more human-centred reason is that it might be unhealthy to eat animals, either for the body, for example, because of the presence in the meat of growth hormones and antibiotics, or for the mind because the animals' fear before death affects our spiritual being.

It doesn't follow that just because it may be unhealthy to eat animals it is morally wrong (although it might still be a good reason for being a vegetarian).

It is possible to feed more people by feeding them grain and vegetables directly than it is by first feeding the grain and vegetables to animals and then feeding the animals to the people. Eating animals may therefore be an uneconomical way for people to consume the protein they need when millions of people are hungry or starving.

Although human-centred this is an ethical reason because it takes account of the rights of others.

But large areas of the earth's surface cannot be used for agriculture. They can only support animals such as sheep or goats. In order to make maximum use of the earth's resources, a combination of agriculture and husbandry may be necessary, though it would mean a significant reduction of people's meat consumption to perhaps once or twice a week.

Not everyone agrees on what the term 'meat' means. For example, some vegetarians claim they don't eat meat, but they do eat fish. Isn't fish merely underwater meat?

It is often argued that the human species has evolved on a combination diet – we are omnivores. We are healthy on a diet that includes vegetables and meat, and that is why we should add meat to our diet. Our teeth are made for it. Meat is included in most people's diets worldwide and has been for centuries, therefore eating meat is morally permissible.

But does the fact that some practice has been established for a long period of time make that practice morally right? For example, for thousands of years people have killed each other, but it doesn't follow that killing is justifiable (see Chapter 6). Also, even if our health would otherwise suffer, is that a sufficient reason to justify our eating meat? Wouldn't it be more virtuous to sacrifice a bit of our own health for the sake of the animals' right to live? This would probably be the view of, for example, vegetarians such as Buddhists and Hindus, millions of whom seem healthy enough.

On the other hand, most animals we eat have been specially bred for our consumption. Without this reason for their existence they would never have been there in the first place. Not eating meat would deprive many animals of the possibility of ever existing.

Veganism is a way of life that avoids all forms of exploitation of, and cruelty to, animals for food, clothing, or any other purpose. A vegan's diet excludes all animal produce: meat, fish, eggs, honey and dairy produce. The moral argument against the use of cow's milk, for example, runs like this: to meet the demand for their milk, cows need to be pregnant once a year. Calves that will not produce milk themselves are slaughtered. The cow's milk supply is artificially increased with hormones. These practices are morally unjustifiable because they cause suffering.

What are some possible moral justifications for veganism?

Every creature's pain and pleasure counts and this includes all human and non-human animals that are sentient beings (there is basic equality between all living creatures).

All sentient beings have inherent value and possess it equally and all have an equal right to be treated with respect, to be treated in ways that do not reduce them to objects (as means for other ends).

What is meant by 'sentient beings' is crucial for the first justification. Also, the extent to which it makes sense to talk about 'rights' without corresponding 'duties' is questionable.

Believing in the transmigration of souls has clear implications for how we should treat animals. Subscribers to this popular metaphysical theory believe that a person's soul is reborn in a new body, either animal or human. The animal in front of me could be my grandfather.

If the distinction between humans and animals is one of degree rather than kind it could be argued that because it is morally right to eat animals it is also morally right to eat humans. However, most agree that it is wrong to kill humans for their meat. If on the other hand, the only means of survival, say after a plane crash, would be to eat your dead fellow passengers, would this be morally wrong?

Would it be helpful to make a distinction between eating people who are already dead, and killing people to eat? In the latter case, we would have to kill the people first, and as such the moral dilemma would shift from examining whether it was right for us to eat them to whether it were right for us to kill them in the first place.

Pets are somehow exceptional animals. We have promoted those animals to be part of our moral community. They are loved and cared for, sometimes as if they were humans. For some, the western treatment and depiction of certain animals reeks of sentimentality. Roger Scruton calls our relationship with pets an 'exception' but also 'in a sense a perversion' and a 'temptation too'.

Although we might have a moral responsibility towards our pet rabbit, to express our moral duty of care to a wild rabbit in the same way would be wrong and not beneficial for wild animals, Scruton claims. After all, we have to take into account not only moral duties to *individual* animals, but also our duty to species. Because a pet rabbit depends entirely on its owner for its survival, we should protect it and feed it. But we don't own wild rabbits, and this changes significantly our duty of care to them. Similarly our duty to our own children differs from our duty to other people's children.

Scruton seems to tie in the concept of moral *duty* with that of *ownership*. How satisfactory is this? Also, does ownership possibly change our duty of care in extent rather than kind?

There are huge religious and cultural differences in the way in which people view and treat animals. Although horses are pets in the Netherlands, they are also a source of meat. The famous French dish of 'frogs' legs' is *in*famous in Britain. Cows are holy in certain religions.

Some animals, such as apes, seem to have a greater capacity for apparently virtuous behaviour than other higher animals. And elephants are seen as particularly noble animals capable of virtues such as generosity, selflessness, and a 'stoical' attitude to life, as well as an unusual capacity for grief. The Buddha is often depicted in the company of an elephant.

Although Buddhists regard most creatures as being 'in the same karmic boat' most moral and spiritual progress is believed to take place at the human level. This is because animals are assumed to have less capacity for choice of action. Therefore, if they behave virtuously, they are more likely to be expressing their inherited character, or responding to human encouragement, than because they want to be moral.

**On the other hand, this raises the interesting question of who is morally superior – one who instinctively does the right thing, or the one who has to think about it?**

**Some would say that with an elephant at least you know where you stand.**

# 20

# ISSUES OF RACE AND DIFFERENCE

## KOFI'S CHOICE

*'We were slow, hesitant and uncaring and we have learnt nothing from Rwanda'*

*Kofi Annan, Secretary-General, United Nations, on Darfur, Sudan, BBC News.*

Ten years after the Rwandan genocide, the United Nations was again faced with a case of genocide based on racial differences. The Arab-dominated Government of Sudan lead a campaign of ethnic cleansing against African Muslim tribes in Darfur, western Sudan. The regime was accused of deliberately impeding humanitarian access to the many hundreds of thousands of African tribal peoples of Darfur who were most at risk.

The violence consisted of organised attacks by militias on civilians and villages, abductions, looting, killings, and rapes.

In order to increase its capacity to fight the Sudan Liberation Army (SLA), the Government of Sudan called for the support of a proxy force made up of ethnic Arab fighters, the Janjaweed. Although the Sudan government probably didn't deliberately set out to target civilians, non-Arabs were systematically targeted.

The Arab militia seemed to find little problem in ill-treating these people, because, by race, they are different.

In *Sophie's Choice*, the author, William Styron – drawing a parallel between the treatment of Jews in Nazi Germany and that of blacks in the US deep south – quotes the story of a young black in Georgia, USA, who is tortured and castrated, and then lynched for allegedly ogling a young white girl. The fact that the girl was physically deformed, and would therefore naturally attract curiosity, and that she was mentally deformed which would make her testimony unreliable, had apparently escaped the notice of the members of the mob that lynched him.

Many lynchings in the American South were not just of poor young blacks daring to whistle at a white girl, but were of affluent business men, a bit like the Jews in Nazi-occupied Europe, who were a threat because they were, through their affluence, becoming too powerful, and generating envy. But most were simply based on abuse of power, a sense of white superiority, and a fear of difference.

**It is this fear that underpins racism. It is the fear that superiority (supremacy) based on racial difference is vulnerable to challenge, and to being demolished intellectually.**

## Vive la différence

Observing differences is part of the search for truths and for meanings – for understanding the world. Yet, concern with difference can be a heavy burden.

Individual differences, whether physical – of size, face, hair, sex, skin colour, shape, ability – or cultural – of language, dress, religion, social class, nationality, gender – enormously influence how we regard ourselves and how others treat us.

Societies seem to operate with dominant notions of what is 'normal' and what is different. While we struggle to conform to the norms of the various groups to which we belong, we simultaneously strive to be individual.

When you look at what humans have in common, you find that differences that are so often emphasised are actually quite small.

And how different are you from yourself over time? Every single cell of your body is replaced within seven years.

Differences among people lend meaning to their lives yet also provoke conflict – conflict between individual differences and conflict between the need to conform versus the need to be different. The pressure to conform to social norms can be irresistible and we are often prepared to give up our individual sense of identity in order to be accepted by the group. We are prepared to wear a uniform, agree to rules, behave like others in the same group. For example, we might wear a suit for work, wear the colours of the favourite sports club, go on mass protest marches.

To function as humans we seem to need, on the one hand, to 'belong' or to be attached to others and, on the other hand, to believe that there is no other person quite like us. To function in the world we have devised elaborate and complex systems of classification and languages that can describe subtle nuances of similarity and difference.

In the pursuit of knowledge, classification systems play a critical part. The values that underpin them are sometimes hidden or taken for granted. But these systems in themselves are open to question. How we define differences between things and how we describe the world is a matter of choice and a matter of language. And the terms and systems we use determine in turn the ways in which we think about the concepts. Often we classify things according to their function for us humans, for example, pets/other animals, edible mushrooms/poisonous mushrooms.

Twentieth century social psychologists were preoccupied with research into social conformity. They thought it might help to explain and prevent cruel and inhumane behaviour between people. Experimental studies sought to gain insight into the kinds of conditions that lead individuals to go along with the dominant social norms of the group, even when this involves violence towards others.

Under what conditions would 'ordinary' people become capable of torture? On the other hand, what makes some people cling to their own beliefs or values in the face of huge pressure to conform to the values of the group; and what gives them the strength to do it?

In the face of contradictory pressures, it is sometimes difficult to know how to conform. For example, on the one hand, policy makers, community leaders and politicians emphasise the country's multiculturalism, and English schools teach about several different religious faiths. On the other hand, the law insists that these same schools organise and impose Christian worship.

The law makes provision for individuals to be treated quite differently according to things like their age, sexuality, mental health, or marital status. Not all citizens are equal in the eyes of the law.

Our outward appearance – how we dress – reflects the need to conform and to be different. In western culture, fashion can exist only by continuously reinventing what is considered attractive or modern. So we have to keep changing how we look and what we wear to remain fashionable. At the same time, we want to stand out from the crowd. Someone 'cool' doesn't dress exactly like everyone else but is out of the ordinary – although not too different. The desire to be different is kept within the boundaries of the normal.

In love and friendship too we want the same but different. We are often drawn towards those we perceive to have different qualities to ours, those differences, perhaps, creating a sense of balance. At the same time, we look for things that we have in common, that can be shared.

For a marriage or partnership to be successful, some would suggest that complementarity is essential; the couple must achieve a balance of skills, qualities and strengths between them. Others argue that it is the differences that provide the spice, energy, and excitement.

On the other hand, marriage vows include the suggestion that certain individual differences will be given up in the interests of the union. This might involve giving up your surname, your religion, your nationality, your bank account, a room of your own.

Working out that we are separate (different?) beings from our mothers is a prerequisite for having a sense of self. In our emotional lives we have to deal with attachment and detachment and these define the difference between what is intimate and familiar and what is separate and strange.

British children are taught that trustworthiness is determined by whether a person is familiar or 'strange'. Britain's 'stranger danger' campaign gives children the message that people they do not know pose the greatest risks to their safety. This is in stark contrast to heroic legends and some of the best known religious stories that emphasise the virtue of being a Good Samaritan – helping others you don't know. It also conflicts with statistical evidence that suggests that close friends and family members can present as much if not more danger to children as strangers can.

The Chinese *Yin-Yang* concept is often quoted in discussions about difference. It is largely understood as representing 'difference' in terms of polarised opposites. This is quite wrong. *Yin* and *Yang* are two aspects of one unity. Each contains within it the seed of the other. Where one increases the other decreases, when one reaches its peak, the other emerges.

*Yin-Yang* refers to two opposing yet complementary aspects of everything in the universe. They are symbols that serve as a metaphorical scaffold on which to build understanding and aid description. They are not found 'out there'. For example, *Yang* is a paradigm of a theoretical maleness – and *Yin* of femaleness – which in their pure form do not exist in nature.

A line from an old blues song says it all – *I bin down so long, it looks like 'up' to me.* When we talk about 'up' (which is *yang*) this is meaningful only when we relate it to 'down' (*yin*). 'Up' and 'down' are two opposing yet complementary aspects of space, which give meaning to each other. If there were no 'down' there would be no 'up'. According to *Yin-Yang*, the same can be said of all universal phenomena since the 'Big Bang', and to ideas such as good/bad and right/wrong.

Chinese philosophers, especially Taoists, regard a dualistic perspective such as 'either right or wrong; either mental or physical' as a gross human error. Perhaps the dualistic mistakes on which so many differences are based are due to the human error of basing concepts on the metaphorical language they have invented to describe phenomena, rather than basing them on empirical observation of those same phenomena.

Wherever there are differences there are similarities. It's a question of emphasis. There are many differences between humans and higher animals, but these are hugely outweighed by the similarities, including the capacity for physical and mental suffering. Losing sight of such similarities rests on the tendency to classify differences on an either/or basis – either you're black or you're white – rather than on the basis of difference by degree.

**Compared with the very few differences, the similarities between Afro-Caribbean people and white Caucasians are vast. The claim that superiority and discrimination can be based on such small differences is barefaced sophism.**

### Race – The long view

*I am not an Athenian or a Greek, but a citizen of the world.*

*Socrates, 470-399 BC.*

When considering racial issues it is worth remembering that most of the world's oldest cultures were not white Caucasian. Contrary to popular myth, the Europeans didn't discover them and civilise them. They were already civilised. Which was often what made them worth colonising.

Cultural diversity outside Europe dates back to long before colonialism. Indigenous societies colonised at different times, by different colonial powers, were extremely diverse in their socio-economic structures and their cultures. These ranged from the subsistence society of the South American Mundurucu, to complex imperial states like the South American Incas and the Indian Mughal Empire. On top of that there was considerable cultural diversity within individual countries. In this respect they were no different from European nations. Try defining what is typically British, or typically European.

And if culture is diverse within just one country, surely

within a whole 'world' it must be highly fragmented; especially in the non-European world, parts of which have been cultural melting pots for thousands of years.

Most non-European countries have been, and still are, the meeting places of many cultures, and not just since the arrival of European colonialists. Many pre-colonial societies were already of mixed cultures – India, for example. And even the European colonists and settlers themselves came from different circumstances and cultures.

The slave trade played an important role in throwing together many diverse cultures – and not just Africans with American colonists. Slave labour in the New World was of all colours and religions. The first indentured workers in the Caribbean were Scots and Irish.

The enormous cultural diversity within English speaking countries takes no account of the even more varied differences of art and culture when you include areas formerly controlled by other colonial powers, such as France, Holland and Spain, and whether they ruled directly or indirectly.

It is difficult to imagine any common thread between, for example, a Vietnamese poet and one from industrialised Brazil. And what would they themselves think about it? Could they identify with each other on the grounds of being non-European?

However, there are 'common threads' imposed from outside on peoples from former colonies. These often emerge through literature. Sometimes they merely touch on existing cultures, remaining separate, parallel. Sometimes they fuse with them to bring about something new.

They include the effect of European materialism and customs, Christian missionary zeal, and the cultural fusion between Christianity and pagan practices that resulted. Other common issues include slavery, indentured labour, and peasant dispossession to feed the capitalist labour market, use of a European language as *lingua franca* (language carries culture with it), and local use of the colonial language as a symbol of elite status.

Literature from most former colonies deals with the effect of colonial education. In some cases the colonial language was withheld for fear that educated natives might become too demanding, or even subversive; elsewhere, local students were forbidden to speak their own tongue on the grounds that the imperial language and culture were superior.

Other common threads include escape from hardship, domination, and exploitation, the effect of merging cultures, and the role of women.

Yet 'hardship' and 'domination' are 'all world' subjects, dealt with by 'developed' world literature from Solzhenitsyn to Steinbeck. Similarly, the role of women has been of European concern as far back as Jane Austen and the Brontë sisters. And a look at Erskine Caldwell alone reveals that relationships between different groups, and race and culture clash, is far from exclusively Third World terrain.

What is regarded as 'Third World' hangs heavily on the values and prejudices of those judging the issue; and the prevailing stereotypes confronting them. Many may regard Third World issues as concerning black people, in poor, tropical, backward, traditional, non-industrialised, or disaster-struck lands. Others may Eurocentrically regard all those 'out there' as having merely *primitive* culture in common.

Despite a common ethos of unified humanity, there is a long history of certain groups – usually whites – harbouring feelings of superiority over other races. Why?

There have been various theories. Evidence for racial inferiority has been sought in *The Bible*. There has been an appeal to evolution with the hypothesis that differing cultures are evidence of earlier, more primitive, stages in human development.

The relatively recent *Modernisation Theory*, which has had the support mainly of Americans, regards western modernisation as *the* model for world development. Dating from the Cold War, it emphasises individualism and innovation, condemns traditional society, and neatly justifies export of American consumerism.

It completely ignores the fact that any existing culture needs to be understood as the product of its own local history, which may, for several reasons, divert from the path of other cultures such as those of Europe and the United States.

Asserting the superiority of western culture, has long justified imperial domination. Whereas in previous empires, merchants provided luxury goods to a wealthy elite at home, the colonial wealth of new empires went into transformation of production processes at home as part of the industrial revolution.

European imperialism provided raw material sources for capitalist enterprises and opened up new markets for their goods. This is reflected in the current economic dependence of developing countries.

Whereas until the 15th century different empires had developed independently, capitalism became a world system. European expansion united the world, but also divided it.

How did small numbers of Europeans control large populations of whole societies? It is often assumed that they must in some way have been superior. The answer is that the history of colonialism is basically one of military conquest – of superior might.

But that wasn't all. What followed was more than mere military occupation. It fed largely on *technical superiority*. If one society is technologically more advanced than another it is financially richer, better organised, has superior weaponry, and can therefore impose its will on others. *Technological superiority* can also imply that the colonisers belong to a different sort of society from the colonised, and that the colonisation may improve the colonised area.

*Technological development* can imply *moral superiority* to justify colonialism in the inevitable march of progress (similar to the *Modernisation Theory*). Acceptance of the superiority of European culture held non-Europeans in a lengthy psychological subordination. The negative stereotypes promulgated by the colonial powers as justification for their occupation came to be accepted by the colonies themselves.

Technical supremacy was not the result of sheer native genius of the industrialised nations, but of three centuries of increasing prosperity and investment initiated by the conquest of Latin America and further financed by plunder from India, and profits from the slave trade, and the West Indies slave plantations.

In India and Africa the gradual extension of power together with the initially rather limited demands made upon the local population meant that colonial peoples sometimes hardly realised they had become subject to imperial authority until it was too late to do anything about it.

**The inferior position they found themselves in – economically and politically – in no way implied cultural inferiority, nor that people in the colonies were in any sense inferior to Europeans as human beings.**

## *Dilemma Training* and race

The Dutch police have undergone *Dilemma Training*, and a major constabulary in Britain is reviewing the possibility of conducting a programme to get to grips with race relations issues. It is seen as a means to raise consciousness about how people of various cultures can be valued in the workplace and the community, and given equal access to opportunities. The method is used to help members of the police force to internalise moral decision making when faced with such issues.

The training helps to open up for discussion the moral dilemmas in organisations surrounding issues connected with ethnic minorities, such as those concerned with recruitment (for example, diversity and positive discrimination). But it can also help to break through the smoke screen of political correctness towards racial and ethnic issues.

An important advantage is that the moral assumptions that disguise the real moral question, for example, political correctness or alleged racism – 'we are always discriminated against' – are replaced by a moral enquiry. This breaks through the stalemate that often surrounds 'racial equality' because these moral assumptions are sidelined during the enquiry process. The fact that all arguments from all stakeholders are included strengthens the justice of the decision.

The enquiry into these moral decisions is the starting point for constructing a 'racial equality' policy, the establishment of basic values and basic dilemmas (for example, equality and individual rights) and the necessary rules to back them up.

Basically, the training helps every employee in the organisation, whatever their race, colour, or position, to raise questions connected with racial issues. Racial equality is made a cornerstone of the individual moral judgement of each employee, rather than being enforced in a set of rules or code of behaviour.

Because every one is involved whatever their race, it can prove to be the most effective and long-lasting way to build bridges between people of different cultures. Racial prejudice, political correctness and taboos are replaced by integrity.

Taking the lead in world democracy...

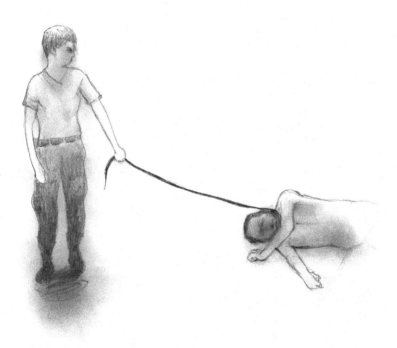

# 21

## MAN VS THE MACHINE – A DILEMMA

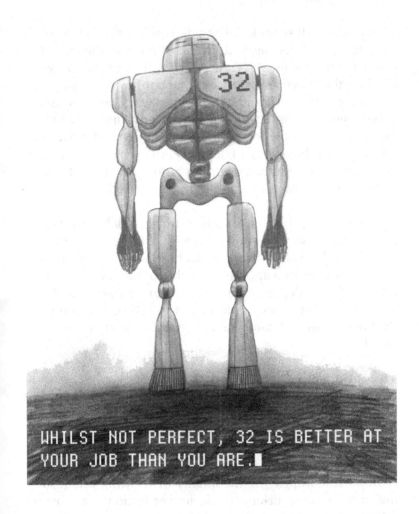

WHILST NOT PERFECT, 32 IS BETTER AT YOUR JOB THAN YOU ARE.

There has been much debate over the past 200 years on the effects of mechanisation in the workplace, and its influence on the quality of working life. The debate for the past 20 years has focused on the effects of *Information and Communication Technology* (ICT).

Viewpoints still seem to be as polarised as they were after introduction of new agricultural machinery in the late 18th century. The pessimistic view is that mechanisation in general is at the expense of jobs, and that application in particular centralises power and control over work, and increases supervision of employees. This, say the pessimists, will undermine job satisfaction, worker autonomy and creativity. The optimists believe ICT enables reorganisation of work to boost efficiency, increases worker autonomy and job satisfaction, and promotes greater individual freedom.

In this chapter, those in favour of Man are labelled 'pessimists' and those who support the Machine are 'optimists'. The choice between Man and Machine is an ethical one – a choice between two apparently right courses of action. The final decision depends on rigorous examination of both sides of the issue, and could produce a choice from one of the horns of the dilemma, or a position somewhere near the middle.

**The optimists**

The optimists believe ICT improves individual freedom and provides greater autonomy and satisfaction for workers. It preserves the best aspects of existing working conditions while avoiding their failings. It attains higher work efficiency while improving the quality of working life, resulting in a shorter working week, longer holidays and early retirement.

They claim that new technology always produces new wealth, which stimulates demand for goods, which creates new jobs; and that ICT is no exception. All technology revolutions eventually produce a net increase in employment, they say.

The optimists say ICT can achieve a return to people-centred work. The machine can serve the worker by being paced to his natural work tempo. Use of industrial robots relieves workers of monotonous, dirty, strenuous and even dangerous work in difficult conditions. As technology develops, machines are becoming increasingly 'user-friendly' – able to be operated without the operator needing formal training in computer use.

In offices and factories, instead of executing a small number of steps in a chain of production specialised according to the principle of division of labour, each worker can handle the entire chain but on a smaller scale.

ICT raises worker participation in planning and decision making. In many areas of work, each employee can become fully accountable to the customer, and have a feeling of direct responsibility, with the consequent feedback and job satisfaction. It can also totally revolutionise the kind of hierarchical managerial structures still prevailing in Europe.

The fact that ICT knowledge has a high obsolescence rate means that staff need regular training for new functions. Rapid developments in ICT open up new careers. This variety makes work more stimulating, and relieves the monotony of performing the same function for too long.

In the new post-industrial society created by ICT, the Protestant work ethic becomes redundant as the needs of labour are reduced to a minimum. This in turn relieves the stigma and loss of self-esteem for those whose jobs have been lost to ICT automation.

New computer technology is eminently suited to closely monitoring various aspects of work. It enables measurement of the pace of work, the number of errors and where they occur, and the operator's absence from the machine. This information enables management to improve work systems and conditions to the benefit of employees' quality of working life, and consequently to their firm's performance.

The computer can also relieve routine work in the skilled professions. The internet can be used to supplement a specialist's own knowledge and experience. Computer systems can even relieve the workloads of doctors, psychologists and others involving routine interviewing. Such systems can ask patients to answer questions to establish their symptoms. The machines, designed to be 'patient-friendly', transcend social and intellectual barriers between doctor and patient, and can be more successful in eliciting honest answers from the patient.

Portable laptops and terminals can promote decentralisation of control, by releasing the worker from the need to be at a certain workplace. They eliminate the need to commute to work, to live near a central office, and can provide work to disabled people, and others unable to leave their homes because of family commitments. Data storage facilities can also enable more flexible working times. The worker can organise his own time and decide where and when he wants to work. Fears of misuse of computerised personnel records can be alleviated by enforcement of effective data protection legislation. Some see the use of ICT to enable establishment of decentralised, consensus-run enterprises as an effective means to avoid more totalitarian control of work.

Word processing on a personal computer (PC) is a good example of where ICT has accelerated the output of work, enabled reductions in manning, and removed the drudgery of routine work. It carries out the more disagreeable, repetitive tasks, while leaving the user free to be more creative.

Computerisation in offices has led to staff cuts, but those that remain benefit from a marked improvement in the quality of their working life.

The use of programmable industrial robots has relieved much of the drudgery and health risk for workers in automobile plants. Robots have for some time now taken over the strenuous work of spot welding on car production lines. A new, and even more important development to working life in a car plant is the introduction of computerised robots for paint spraying. This relieves workers from operating in an unsatisfactory environment of high temperature and humidity, on tasks that are strenuous, repetitive, dull and dangerous to health.

Robots do the work more cheaply and more efficiently, leaving decision making and troubleshooting work to humans. This improves worker satisfaction, and competitiveness of the producer. Resultant growth of the firm should guarantee preservation of existing employment levels, and possibly creation of new jobs. This in turn can promote a feeling of greater job security among workers.

**The pessimists**

The pessimists warn of massive unemployment, de-skilling, and centralised power and control of the workplace. There is a progressive loss of work autonomy, job satisfaction and creativity. Employment for fewer people leading to even greater centralisation of information is likely to make a bad job worse, increase control over the worker, devalue skills and make work more boring. With the aid of computers, jobs can be broken down even more into component parts. Only those a machine cannot handle will be left to humans. It will restrict manual, clerical, and even some professional work to an even greater extent. This isolates workers from the rest of the work process, reduces creativity and motivation, and increases worker alienation and conflict.

Highly skilled and professional people can lose their independence to the computer. Their jobs can become dominated by vast computer databases of knowledge and computer programmes which, without the benefit of extensive computer training, are beyond their grasp. The complexity of computer systems causes anxiety and frustration if they outrun their users' intellectual capacity. Training by computer for highly responsible jobs – for example, physician or airline pilot – can neglect first-hand experience in the real world, and the ability to cope with unforeseeable events.

Many pessimists assume that the use of technology in the labour process will be determined by the existing economic system, comprising the goals of industry and commerce. The ultimate goal of production, basically unchanged since the emergence of capitalism, is to maximise profits, not to meet human needs. This goal will be furthered by introduction of ICT.

They assume that it is management's aim to control every aspect of the worker's life on the job. Computer technology is eminently suited to this end, and often used accordingly. Computerisation makes possible a degree of supervision and control never before realised. The pace of work, number of errors, and absence from the machine can be closely monitored and recorded.

Investment in expensive computerised office equipment can lead to demands for shift work for office workers as employers try to get the highest return on their investment. They may offer work at home on portable terminals under the guise of providing workplace flexibility, but only to encourage black economy part-time work, or piecework without job security. Working at home can also put a strain on marriages and families; and it eliminates the social function and structured hours of the workplace. Some people can manage without their time being structured, but many cannot.

There are a number of health and safety problems associated with using screens, such as eyestrain and fatigue. There are fears that security agencies can gain access to personnel files on records of work, psychological tests, and medical details stored by the company doctor. And employers can use their terminals to access confidential information on employees, such as past medical history and credit worthiness.

There is no reason to believe that existing economic theory will work in the post-industrial society. ICT automation *does* raise efficiency and production levels, and *does* increase demand. But in contrast with the past, it does not necessarily create new jobs. Jobs could also be lost in small enterprises that cannot afford to keep up with ICT developments. This would concentrate multinational big business, and increase centralisation and control of labour. Older people, who fail to adapt to changes brought about by ICT in the workplace, will become unemployable.

Typically women's jobs in offices and factories are the first to be automated. The computer industry *has* provided new jobs done mainly by women. But they are similar to the old unpleasant production line tasks it set out to eliminate – the fiddly piecing together of component parts of computer hardware.

Accelerated obsolescence in ICT knowledge and skills means workers have to undergo frequent retraining for new functions. This can cause stress, and fear of unemployment, with consequent psychological and economic strain. Workers can feel powerless in their inability to anticipate the kind of changes that will occur in ICT development, and their effects on job security and quality. They are even more likely to allow themselves to become the tools of management, rather than making their own career choices.

Workers' fear of increased centralisation and control of the workplace verges on a *Big Brother* syndrome. Workers in any job or profession are anxious and resentful at having someone looking over their shoulder. The 'some*one*' has now been replaced with 'some*thing*' – the microprocessor. It is particularly easy to introduce in office work. Word processors in offices can closely monitor an individual typist's performance by providing reports on arrival time, volume of work done, etc.

Managers have the tendency to fix targets for work output using the average of such performance figures. These put slower workers under considerable pressure, and produce stress and alienation from the work. The typist can have the feeling that he is subservient to the machine, instead of the other way round, and that the machine is spying on him.

It's not just the routine jobs that come under the pressure of centralised control. Middle management may be enthusiastic about the ease of communication via networks and videoconferences. And senior management is delighted at the savings in travel expenses. But those involved are victim to the *desocialising* effect of the new forms of communication, and the resultant degree of *control* over their lives.

Most people find it difficult enough to relax for a few seconds in front of a camera. The thought of communicating with a business associate while every word said and every expression made is going down on permanent record can prove highly stressful to even the most seasoned of communicators. The fact that senior management have immediate access to such records has again increased centralised control, and given the employee the feeling of being watched.

## Conclusion

The pessimists and optimists are probably right and wrong in varying degrees. If the age of microelectronic technology can be seen as a new industrial revolution; and if it is possible to judge from history, then the pessimists are likely to be right in the short term, while lessons are being learned and mistakes made, and the optimists right in the long term once the teething troubles have been solved, and the benefits realised. Meanwhile, the creation of more fragmented jobs would be regarded as a necessary, but temporary evil during the development stage.

This assumes that the present industrial revolution, leading to a post-industrial society, will develop in a similar way to that of the first – the age of steam. But before it reached the stage of providing millions with improved living standards, the steam age had brought to millions the horrors of industrialisation, and carried in its wake tremendous social upheavals and human misery.

The important difference now is that the present revolution is taking place much swifter. The changes in working life resultant upon ICT in the past 20 years have been more extensive than during the whole of 19th century industrialisation. Lessons have already been learned from the past, and are being learned from the present at a much faster rate.

One lesson from the past must be that many of the social horrors of industrialisation could have been ameliorated by government intervention.

The first industrial revolution took workers out of the fields and into the factories. Now ICT has automated the factories, and directed workers into the service industries. The optimists believe higher efficiency of the service industries will lead to their expansion and growth of employment; and that new technologies always produce net increases in employment. The pessimists believe that jobs lost to automation have gone for good, and will not be replaced.

The question is whether this new industrial revolution can be judged in a historical light. In the past, the driving force of industrialisation – steam in the 19th century – has been relatively limited. But this time the driving force is a computer with universal application and potential, leaving nowhere for labour to go after complete automation of the service industries.

There is no common agreement on the impact of ICT on employment and the quality of working life. The optimists are probably *over* optimistic, the pessimists *too* pessimistic.

Job prospects can be seen more optimistically – provided essential social changes take place, and keep pace. These include abandoning the work ethic and the stigma of unemployment; providing adequate income levels for the unemployed – perhaps even a higher income to reward those sufficiently socially responsible to surrender their right to a job in times of high unemployment. And ensuring that wealth created by automated sectors is channelled into provision of leisure activities, education, and other social services.

For those that remain in employment, the quality of working life *could* improve, with more individual freedom, autonomy and worker participation. On the other hand, ICT could be used to intensify centralisation and control of the workplace. There are arguments on both sides. And on most issues the optimist and pessimist views are diametrically opposed. They can't both be right. Is one of them right? Or are they both wrong?

The answer probably is that they are *both right*, but in *very different scenarios*.

These scenarios would be based very much on individual values and beliefs, not only about the technology itself, but in grey areas like human nature, or political and economic theory. Someone who religiously believes in the effectiveness of capitalism and liberal economics, and is convinced that humans are basically lazy and egocentric, will support an entirely different scenario from the person who sees capitalism as unfair exploitation and suppression of the creativity of humans as a highly social species.

Because of the newness of the technology, many of the relevant facts are unknown, and forecasts are mere calculated guesswork. The future impact of ICT on workers depends greatly on management ideology. It is the expectations of management applying ICT that determine whether you adopt the pessimist or optimist standpoint on all the other related issues.

The values and beliefs that managers hold about human nature are likely to guide them in their application of ICT. But the irony is that whatever the choice of application, the philosophy behind it will prove to be a self-fulfilling prophecy. The consequences of the way ICT are introduced to workers and their jobs will tend to confirm the manager's beliefs about human nature.

For example, the manager with a jaundiced view of human nature will use ICT to tighten control over his workforce. This will alienate workers, dampen their goodwill, and tend to bring out the worst in them in performance terms and reliability. This would then confirm the manager's prejudices that led him or her to increase control in the first place.

How ICT is applied in the work place, and its effect on individual freedom, eventually comes down to a question of enlightened choice. But at what level? The pessimists clearly mistrust the intentions and goals at management level.

Although managers are probably capable of sorting out the facts of the technology, together with the validity of economic theories to support its application, it will be up to the government to pass judgement on conflicts of values and beliefs. Its ability to do so will partly depend on the imagination of its economic advisers. One problem is that economists are notoriously traditional in clinging to established economic theories.

**In the post-industrial society, the roles of capital and labour will be diminished to the point where capitalism and socialism lose their meaning. The question is whether politicians and economists will make the huge philosophical leap to enable them to deal effectively with the new order.**

# 22

# DOES THE PUNISHMENT FIT THE CRIME?

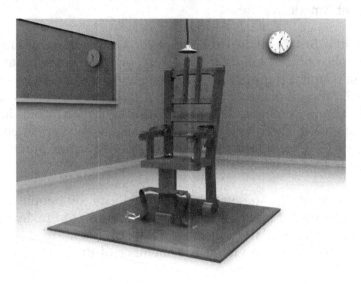

---

*My object all sublime*
*I shall achieve in time –*
*To let the punishment fit the crime –*
*The punishment fit the crime.*

*Gilbert and Sullivan, The Mikado.*

---

The following three chapters deal with some extremely difficult and emotionally painful life and death dilemmas. They are capital punishment vs imprisonment, and euthanasia or suicide vs a life of intolerable suffering.

This chapter looks at the various arguments for and against capital punishment, and then examines the ethics of punishment in general.

## Capital punishment or state murder?

There are those who believe that to eliminate murder it makes sense to eliminate murderers. This is still the case in most American states.

In 1957 Britain abolished hanging for all except murdering a police officer, killing by shooting, or while resisting arrest. Capital punishment was suspended for five years in 1965, and permanently abolished in 1970. And the terms of the country's membership of the European Union forbids its restoration. There have been a number of votes in Parliament since 1970, considering the reintroduction of capital punishment. Each one has been defeated.

Opinion polls suggest that the majority of people in Britain would still like to see the restoration of the death penalty, particularly following a high profile murder case such as when the victim is a member of the police or a child.

Those who want to restore capital punishment for murder argue that:

- it is a deterrent.

- criminals would be less likely to carry guns if there was a threat of their being hanged for killing.

- life imprisonment is a fate worse than death.

Abolitionists argue that:

- other countries have abolished capital punishment without a noticeable increase in crime.

- mistakes have been made and the wrong person executed.

- most murders are crimes of passion, so capital punishment is usually not a deterrent.

- execution in a civilised society is barbaric.

Those that support restoration of capital punishment usually do so in the wake of the killing of a police officer. That was certainly the case following the shooting of a policewoman in Bradford and another policewoman in London during 2005. The standpoint is that the threat of the death penalty would help the police protect the public.

Those who want to bring back hanging also claim that the existence of the death penalty discouraged criminals' use of firearms; and that since abolition of capital punishment, their use has risen. Although few would claim a causal connection between the two factors.

Those in favour suggest that capital punishment provides a threat of retribution for those criminals who carry firearms with the intention of using them. They equate judicial killing (by hanging in Britain) with that of a criminal killing with a gun, and that such a threat would act as a deterrent.

But most murderers are not criminals in the sense of being people who deliberately set out on a life of crime. They become murderers as the result of an unpremeditated act – a temporary lapse of reason.

In cases of terrorism the death sentence might be useless against ideological or political fanatics, and would certainly be no deterrent against those on suicide missions.

Brazilian electrician, Jean Charles de Menezes, was shot dead by anti-terrorist police in July 2005 because he was a suspected suicide bomber. Since 1965 Britain has outlawed the death penalty following a fair trial, but execution without trial is excused as part of the war on terror.

Restorationists' main argument in favour of the death penalty is that it is a deterrent. It runs as follows: most policemen and women are of the opinion that the existence of the death penalty would discourage criminals' use of guns, and deter professional assassins (but has no proven effect on fanatical terrorists). On balance, fewer criminals would use guns, therefore police work would be easier, so protection of the public would be more effective.

There is a second argument – for the death penalty as retribution, justified by comparing a criminal killing, with the imposition of a judicial sentence. However, not only are the two not analogous, but by assuming they are, reversal of the argument produces the uncomfortable conclusion that carrying out the death penalty can be seen as legal murder – state killing – and no different, and therefore, morally no better, than the crime it is supposed to deter. Instead of one murder, there would be two murders (two wrongs).

The major weakness in the argument itself is its apparent reliance on evidence that either is assumed but has not been presented, or which depends on no demonstrable causal link. The argument rests mainly on factual data suggesting there has been a substantial increase in the carrying of firearms by criminals since the abolition of the death penalty. Yet, there is no suggestion that there have been more killings as a result.

Just because they increased *after* abolition, doesn't mean they increased *because* of it. And if they didn't increase because of it, how is reinstatement of the death penalty going to help? There could have been many other reasons for the increased carrying of firearms. There could be an increase because guns are more readily available and are cheaper.

To be effective, a deterrent must weaken the resolve of people to act in a particular way. To achieve this, the people involved have to contemplate the consequences prior to acting. Arguably, this might be the case with certain people acting rationally, but this argument cuts no ice when applied to irrational beings – those, for example, overcome by a fit of jealousy or passion for vengeance.

Apart from being open to the above criticisms, restorationists do not touch on one particular problem with the death penalty – the fact that it is irreversible; and that prosecution evidence and judgement can never be infallible. Never infallible for two reasons – the impossibility of having perfect knowledge of the state of the killer's mind, and of possessing perfect knowledge of the circumstances in which the crime was committed. 'Beyond all reasonable doubt' seems to fall short of what is needed when depriving someone of their life.

But does irreversibility really matter as a ground for reluctance to reintroduce capital punishment? The answer surely depends on what such punishment is meant to achieve. If retribution is aimed for, then of course mistakes count. There is no retribution if the wrong person is punished. But retribution, in itself, won't undo the crime committed, and, at best, only prevents further such crimes by the murderer concerned.

Life imprisonment has the same effect – it prevents the killer from killing again, and at least is reversible. However, if the whole point of retribution is to deter others, then surely it doesn't matter *who* is punished, so long as mistakes are never made public.

It has been suggested from a simple utilitarian viewpoint that there is a 'balance sheet' – one, or perhaps two, innocent lives versus the effect of the death sentence deterring the murder of many more people. It has got a point – from the deterrence point of view. And if you strip out the 'sanctity of life' and 'categorical imperative' considerations contained in deontological ethics (see chapter 6), and you accept that what is 'right' is what is right for the community as a whole, then perhaps, the community's killing of a few innocents to prevent the murder of many more, could be justified – even the killing of a scapegoat – but only if there is no doubt that capital punishment deters.

The capital (and corporal) punishment debate still rages. But whether the death penalty should be reintroduced hinges on a number of vagaries at various levels, none of which, even the most superficial, has been, or, perhaps, can be, resolved. Even at the most elementary level – does capital punishment deter murder? – there are still no firm conclusions. And even if there were a clear causal link between the incidence of the crime and the deterrent effect of the punishment, a further array of questions remains unanswered: what is meant by 'murder' versus manslaughter, crime of passion, killing the 'enemy'? Is killing always wrong? Is killing as a punishment ever right? And finally, to deter, does the punishment have to fit the crime?

Rather than frenetically searching for the facts to fit the deterrence hypothesis, there might be some justification for seeking alternative ways to reduce the murder rate, and meanwhile applying the precautionary principle to capital punishment – while in doubt, leave it out.

**Is it right to punish?**

Punishment is the deliberate infliction of harm by an authority as a moral sanction against perceived offenders. It may be physical, mental, emotional, or social. It can include the withdrawal of something enjoyed by the offender, or consist of harm to the offender.

Who has the authority to decide to deliberately inflict harm on someone? Parents claim that they have the right to punish their children when they misbehave. But what are the limits of that punishment? Is it justifiable to smack your children, and if so, what gives you that right? Is there a moral difference between smacking your own children and smacking other people's? Does a child have a right to hit its parents when they misbehave? It could be claimed that they have the right. Although enforcing that right would be unusual and highly problematic.

Punishing offenders has been ethically justified in several ways. If someone has been harmed in any way, justice seeks to rectify the moral order by taking from the offender and giving to the victim. The main and primary purpose of a punishment, according to this theory, is that the offender suffers pain in proportion to the wrong they have done. Retribution is an end in itself. The desirable outcomes are much less important.

The Old Testament dictum 'An eye for an eye, and a tooth for a tooth' is a retributive justification. This usually satisfies an offender's duty to repair the harm done to the victim. Of course, the exception is when the victim is dead; a life can be taken, but not returned. Retribution also pre-empts the possibility of revenge killings – vendettas – by the victim's friends and family.

The danger of retributive systems is that they can provide a legal outlet for revenge – perhaps even for issues unrelated to the offence. On the other hand, it can be argued that justice is separate from revenge. After all, we can feel outraged by crimes we ourselves are not at all involved in. And sometimes offenders themselves want to be punished.

Punishment would make sense only if the offender had a *choice* of action, taking into account character and circumstances. We can't blame people for their actions if they couldn't have acted differently.

For example, when a child is seriously neglected at home, physically and emotionally, and misbehaves at school, it is questionable as to what extent he could help being rude to the teacher, or stealing from a classmate.

Also, you have to weigh up the advantages and consequences of a retributive approach. For example, if someone steals because they are penniless, it is pointless to fine them. Does it make sense to punish someone if no advantage will be gained, either by the offender or by the victim? The common good, as well as the good of the offender's victim, need to be weighed up carefully and reasonably.

One argument for punishment is that knowledge of the possible penalties involved will deter potential offenders. Also if, by putting someone in prison you make it impossible for that person to reoffend, further crimes will be prevented. In both cases, the desirable outcomes are central to the punishment decision.

For some, the most important reason for punishing people is to improve their moral character, so that they will behave better in future. However, if we prevent people from reoffending because they are fearful of a repetition of the punishment, can we still say they have changed for the right (moral) reasons – that they recognise the wrongness of their actions?

It might prevent reoffending, but the person is still not necessarily moral. Furthermore, some people offend because they believe it is right, or because it is their duty. Punishment will not reform, for example, terrorists or others who commit crimes for political reasons.

Although it is clear that many arguments can be used to justify punishment, you can wonder to what extent it is sometimes simply an instinctive reaction to crime – the need to hit back. A system of punishments can easily be abused and cause physical or psychological damage beyond the level justified by the offence.

In some cases the consequences of breaking the rules can be a punishment in itself. For example, a driver who breaks the speed limit and knocks down and kills a child has to live with the pain of guilt and regret.

It could also be argued that inflicting pain on others is always wrong – and that two wrongs do not make a right. A retributionist could reply that whether something is wrong or not depends on the context, and that painful punishment is justifiable in cases where the offender inflicted pain.

**Despite the Old Testament 'an eye for an eye' dictum, it is widely accepted that two wrongs rarely make a right. Doing unto others what you would *have them do unto you*, rather than what they *actually did to you*, does seem to be a morally superior alternative. Furthermore there is a sense that stooping to act in ways similar to the crime – for example, imposing the death penalty to avenge a murder – lowers the punisher to the moral level of the punished.**

# 23

# EUTHANASIA – LETTING DIE OR KILLING?

*Euthanasia* is the outcome of one of the starkest of dilemmas – to let someone suffer intolerable pain vs to actively help them carry out their wish to die.

The term *Euthanasia* is associated with someone's personal decision to allow their life to end. This is usually associated with terminally-ill patients who have decided that their life is no longer worth living. It is also associated with the Netherlands, where it is legal and widely accepted.

This is known as *voluntary* euthanasia, also known as 'assisted suicide' (see chapter 24). But there is also *involuntary* euthanasia – letting someone die – 'pulling the plug' on someone who no longer seems to have a life worth living but who is incapable of expressing a wish either to live or die.

It was the issue of involuntary euthanasia that, in 2005, led to a challenge in the Court of Appeal by Britain's General Medical Council (GMC) against a ruling in favour of a 45-year-old man with a degenerative brain condition. Leslie Burke had already won a landmark ruling to prevent doctors from withdrawing food and drink when he could no longer speak. Burke feared that, like so many others, he would be condemned to die of thirst – fully conscious, in pain, but unable to swallow for the two weeks it would take him to die.

The GMC Guidelines state that treatment, including artificial feeding, can be discontinued if a patient's condition has deteriorated so severely and the prognosis is so poor that doctors believe it would be 'too burdensome in relation to the possible benefits'. Burke had argued that these guidelines were incompatible with the European Convention on Human Rights, which enshrines a 'right to life'. The ruling gave Burke the right to artificial nutrition even at the point where he could no longer communicate.

Aside from the question of whether feeding is 'treatment' that doctors have the right to withdraw, a patient who is mentally competent should decide where his best interests lie.

On the other hand, it can be argued that it is questionable as to whether patients should have complete discretion over their treatment. If a patient chooses to die or insists on pointless treatment, must a doctor accede to their wishes? The result would be that a patient could require a doctor to provide a form of treatment that the doctor considered of no clinical benefit. It could also be inconsistent with the Hippocratic oath that doctors take committing them to save life.

The Catholic Bishops Conference of England and Wales said Leslie Burke's ruling elevates the principle of autonomy to an 'absolute', so that in the provision of life-prolonging treatment, doctors must regard the patient's wishes as simply 'determinative'.

The case raises profound ethical questions about the dividing line between personal autonomy and the duty of doctors to act in what they regard as their patients' best interests.

More profoundly, it highlights the need to examine whether there really is any distinction between letting someone die or just killing them.

## Killing vs letting die

Letting someone die is not much different from killing them. It can be seen as simply killing them more slowly.

Chapter 4 touched upon the issue of killing vs letting die, and suggested that the latter was an excuse – hypocrisy – to sidestep the difficult, and possibly illegal, decision to end someone's life when they clearly demand it, or, if they can no longer communicate when their life has obviously become unbearable.

This also raises the question of *acts and omissions*. Does an omission carry the same ethical responsibility as an act? In other words, is the moral content of your actions the same as that of your inaction. For example, if you send a cheque to the Tsunami fund, you will be responsible for saving lives. If you do not send a cheque, are you responsible for the loss of those same lives?

In law, the difference usually hinges on proof of negligence. If you neglect to maintain safety standards at work, you could be held responsible for any accidents. If you have food and water, and neglect to prevent someone for whom you are responsible, from dying from starvation or thirst, you are culpable.

Is the case of killing as against letting die one of difference between acts and omissions – a case for fine philosophical argument? Not really. The difference isn't simply one of actively treating the patient to keep them alive versus not treating them. It is a case of medically treating them vs failing to give them the basics that any person needs to stay alive – food and drink.

You can kill somebody (quickly) by giving them a lethal injection, and you can also kill them (slowly) by starving.

In a different context, for example that of Auschwitz, there would be no doubt that starving somebody to death (against their wishes) would be murder. If, however, people have clearly expressed their wish to die, then killing them could amount to mercy killing. And if you can choose between killing quickly and killing slowly, then quickly is surely the more merciful.

There have been several court cases on the subject of involuntary euthanasia. One interesting landmark case in Britain concerned a Down's syndrome child, who had been 'let die' by his surgeon. The case is particularly interesting, not only because it involves the killing vs 'letting die' dilemma, but also because it concerns someone who was not terminally ill. It concerns a child who was born with an intestinal obstruction, which, if not removed, meant he would die.

The surgeon found himself in court to defend his actions, which were finally upheld by the presiding judge.

During the court hearing the judge commented: '…the surgeon might say: "As this child is a mongol [sic]… I do not propose to operate; I shall let nature take its course". No one could say that the surgeon was committing an act of murder by declining to take a course of action which would save the child.'

It may well be that the judge would have expressed a different view if the child had been 'normal'. In which case the conclusion would be: therefore declining to take a course of action that would save a *Down's syndrome* child is not an act of murder.

Much hangs on the distinction between killing and letting die – between active and passive euthanasia – the former being manslaughter or murder, and the latter being something else. In this case, the surgeon did something else – he let die, rather than kill, and therefore was not 'committing an act of murder'. That distinction applies in law, but is it valid morally?

In view of the fact that there was no untreatable life-threatening condition, the decision to opt for non-treatment amounted to intentional ending of life (i.e. killing). The judge must have agreed that the baby was 'better off dead, and that the doctor acted in the baby's best interests'. Objections that the decision was disrespectful of autonomy might have been upheld on the grounds that the baby would have been unable to autonomously express any preferences, although this does not mean that he had no right to autonomy.

But what about the rights and wishes of other stakeholders? In most such cases these would include the parents. In this case, the mother was a single parent who had expressed the wish that her baby should not be saved. There were no known stakeholders who had an interest in his survival. He was simply unwanted.

What about the moral distinction between killing and letting die? Is there one, really? No, say several, mainly utilitarian philosophers. American philosopher James Rachels, for example, argues that the distinction (active vs passive euthanasia) has no moral (as opposed to legal) significance whatsoever – that they amount to the same thing, that is bringing death to someone.

Moral judgements usually take account of intention. The intention in letting die, and killing, is identical – that the patient be dead. And, for supporters of the concept of negative responsibility – responsibility for the consequences of inaction (passive) is no different from those arising from actions (active).

Rachels doesn't explicitly state that active euthanasia is morally okay either; he just says that if passive euthanasia is morally acceptable, then so is the active variety. This is not a moral licence to kill. The implication is: killing is the same as letting die; killing is morally (and legally) not permissible; therefore letting die is not permissible. If the surgeon was not permitted to kill the baby, he should not have been allowed to let him die either. On the other hand, if he was allowed to let him die, he should have been allowed to kill him.

The 'nursing care only' regime prescribed for the baby was such that no person could survive under it. Was it 'letting die'; or was it 'killing' by starvation? Either way the surgeon was causally responsible for the child's death. The difference is that the course of action he chose was not the quickest, and therefore, not the most humane.

Assuming that humane action is morally correct, and assuming that humane action is clearly identifiable, then the surgeon's action was less correct morally than it could have been. Morally speaking, having decided the child should not live, he could have killed him. One ameliorating factor here is that it is also considered immoral to break the law (in most cases), and overtly killing the baby would have done so in a major way.

Relying on the distinction between killing and letting die to deny the right to perform euthanasia looks like a cop-out. It is almost analogous to splitting the difference between lying and not telling the truth – both deceive, both undermine confidence in good faith, both trigger suspicion about intentions. (In Sartre's terms [see below], someone falling back on this distinction for the sake of avoiding the responsibility of taking action would be acting in 'bad faith'.)

The judge might also have considered the 'double effect' doctrine. This might have been used to argue that the decision not to operate was primarily intended to prevent further suffering – the baby's, his mother's, the state's and other stakeholders' – and that death was an unfortunate side-effect. Undoubtedly, the doctrine is an effective comfort to help doctors do what they know they 'ought' to do, and convince themselves (and/or others), that they intended something else. For example, prescribing morphine painkillers to terminal cancer patients is doubly effective – overtly to relieve pain, covertly to hasten death. But its use is vulnerable to accusations of hypocrisy, and also of abuse (which is why it is so difficult to legislate on the issue).

A utilitarian justification for letting the baby die would be that his life would have been of such low quality that the amount of happiness it would bring him would be minimal, compared with the lack of happiness for his mother and the medical staff who would have to care for him. (The mother rejected the baby after birth.)

The utilitarian might say that if the baby lived, the parents would suffer the lack of happiness due to mental pain and physical inconvenience, and that the medical profession would lose the happiness of being able to employ elsewhere the resources that would be tied up caring for him.

On the other side of the equation, the baby has to surrender his entire stock of happiness, however minimal. The problem here is the typically utilitarian one of measuring and comparing happiness. What sort of criteria are there to help make correct and accurate judgements of this sort?

Not only do attitudes towards killing vary across cultures and time – so do (closely connected) attitudes to death. Is death good, bad, or simply non-existence, and therefore neutral? But that surely depends on the life concerned? Judgement of morality of euthanasia needs to examine just what euthanasia would be offering the patient – and that depends (partly) on the kind of life he has. But who is to judge, and how?

There is a sense that not all problems can be solved using purely reason, and its tool, logic. Empathy – putting yourself in someone else's shoes – is a useful aid to ethical decision making. Did the judge put himself in the surgeon's and/or the baby place? Did the surgeon himself try to imagine, to feel, what it would be like to be the baby? Was the decision to let die, and the judgement to absolve liability, influenced by such empathy? Who knows? But if they were, how did the judge and doctor know how much of themselves to put into the baby's place? How could they decide which of their values, preferences and expectations were appropriate, and which to leave aside? This would involve being able to make correct judgements about what that life is going to be like. How were they to judge?

A further distinction is the difference between the use of ordinary and extraordinary means to maintain life. The American Medical Association (AMA), for example, accepts only that extraordinary means be discontinued when '...there is irrefutable evidence that biological death is imminent...' Since the intensity of the baby's treatment is unclear, the ordinary/extraordinary criteria cannot be applied here (which does save arguing about how to distinguish between 'ordinary' and 'extraordinary').

But, there is a problem – in this case, imminent biological death was from intestinal obstruction, quite independently of Down's syndrome. Yet, the judge's summing up says, '...the surgeon might say: "As this child is a mongol... I do not propose to operate..."'.

Being a 'mongol' is not, in itself, life-threatening. And an intestinal obstruction can be surgically corrected. The judge would have had to accept that having Down's syndrome *and* having intestinal obstruction together make biological death imminent. But they don't, any more than an intestinal obstruction together with being an unwanted 'normal' child is life-threatening.

While Down's syndrome children without intestinal problems are allowed to live, and while babies with intestinal
problems, but without Down's syndrome are treated, the
conclusion must be that the baby was allowed to die for
some other reason. He died – not because of an untreatable
life-threatening condition – but as the result of the decision
not to treat it. That looks like non-voluntary euthanasia. If
Rachels is right – 'if letting die' equals 'killing' (slowly, in
this case) – then the baby was *killed* for some reason other
than to save him suffering ahead of imminent death. But
that would look like grounds for a murder charge.

**Be yourself and be damned**

So, why did the surgeon do it? Attempts to solve the problems about how to act correctly do seem to have taken the
form of a sort of system building – structures as references to
help decide logically and reasonably what is the right thing
to do. These have thrown up a number of vagaries, many
of which need case-by-case interpretation, which itself can
be arbitrary. They include involuntary vs non-voluntary vs
voluntary euthanasia; active vs passive; doctrine of double
effect; extraordinary vs ordinary treatment; the doctrine of
negative responsibility – smoke screens dividing responsibility from action from consequences?

To paraphrase Robert Pirsig, author of *Zen and the Art of
Motorcycle Maintenance*, the ethics of reason seem to direct
the agent to a restaurant with a bible-thick menu, but no
food. Something very essential seems to be missing. The
intellectual meanderings produce a sort of disengagement.
So, what is missing from the whole picture as to why the
surgeon let the baby die – empathy perhaps? But, what is
empathy? – a 'trying to put yourself in someone else's shoes'
type of thought experiment – or more than that? And if
more, can the 'more' be discussed in rational terms?

Where empathy is possible, the resultant (possibly spontaneous) action might be so idiosyncratic as to conflict with

law, reason or established rules of morality, and pit the agent against all the weight of disapprobation that society can bring to bear. What then?

Particularly relevant in the context of ethical decision making, a look at French existential philosopher, Jean-Paul Sartre (1905-1980), provides more than just rationality. The basis of his philosophy is that all individuals have absolute responsibility for everything they are and do. Most people avoid such ultimate responsibility by playing a role as though their actions were predestined, or morally correct. In Sartre's terms, such people act in 'bad faith' (see Chapter 24). 'Good faith' comprises the attempt to behave in ways that involve no self-deception – by thinking and acting in ways true to oneself without even doing so self-consciously.

Moral values to judge right actions are supra-individual, have a sort of independent existence, and involve the sort of role-playing that stands in the way of self-realisation, and the 'authentic' choices that go with it. For the agent to carry out, or not carry out, euthanasia in the role of, for example, a 'law abiding citizen', rather than as a freely chosen act, would be to act in what Sartre calls 'bad faith'.

In Sartre's terms, there are no excuses – no intellectual smokescreens – for avoiding the responsibility of absolute freedom. You can never excuse your actions by denying the freedom to act in a particular way on the grounds that the act would be 'against the law', 'not doing my duty'; nor even that it would be 'immoral'. However unpleasant the consequences, you always have the power to make any of the choices of action available. There is no such thing as 'cannot' – only 'will not'.

If values (the moral 'oughts') are not somehow given – are just projections onto the world to help cope with life and death within it – then there are no moral 'facts' – no Kant-like 'categorical imperatives' (except, of course, to never act in bad faith). Sartre's ethical code – for want of a more appropriate expression – is that there are no codes; only personal responsibility.

Killing someone could be, morally, the least bad of a set of worse options, whatever the law threatens, or whatever social and religious conventions prescribe. In Sartre's view, a person who, true to himself, carries out a mercy killing, perhaps based on an 'authentic' reaction to empathy for the patient, will be acting in 'good faith', morally.

The surgeon brought about the death of the baby. If the judge had concluded that the doctor had 'killed' the baby, he would have been a 'murderer' before the law and prevailing morality. But if this 'murder' had been carried out in 'good faith', perhaps out of empathy for the baby and/or his parents, the surgeon would, in Sartre's terms, have been a 'mercy killer', not a murderer. The judgement would depend on examining the criteria on which he based his decision. And, whatever his criteria, another question is whether he should have been the sole judge?

**But, anyway, he didn't kill, he let die; and the judge decided that, 'No one could say that the surgeon was committing an act of murder...' Okay. But even if he had acted in 'good faith' in causing the baby's death, his 'letting die' rather than 'killing' – perhaps in the role of a 'law-abiding citizen' – reflects an avoidance of personal responsibility, which, according to Sartre, might protect him from a charge of murder, but still exposes him to a charge of serious 'bad faith'.**

# 24

# THE ULTIMATE DILEMMA

# TO BE OR NOT TO BE

---

*'There is but one truly serious philosophical problem, and that is suicide. Judging whether life is or is not worth living amounts to answering the fundamental question of philosophy.'*

*Albert Camus, 1913-1960.*

---

There are some ethical dilemmas that force you into choices that just cannot be lived with. Two years after the end of the war, still haunted by her awful choice, Sophie and her New York Jewish boyfriend, who cannot bear to live without Sophie, enter a suicide pact. They curl up in bed together, in a lovers' embrace both facing the same direction, and take a lethal dose of sodium cyanide.

The author's own grandmother, having lost five of her nine children, living with the guilt of secretly giving up a love child to adoption, and losing her husband in a train accident, struggled alone to bring up the remaining children in poverty. Probably exhaustion and worry wore her down, and she finally killed herself.

In the context of their suffering, how can such people be said to have acted unethically?

French existentialist philosopher and novelist, Albert Camus (1913-1960), survived German occupation, despite editing an underground resistance newspaper. Camus claimed that *suicide* is the one true philosophical problem. This is not a prescription to avoid difficult choices, but points out the fact that whether to continue to live is itself ultimately the most fundamental choice you can make. He maintained that this ability to choose is essential to an authentic existence, in which you can feel in charge of your life rather than being a victim of circumstances.

There is an abundance of literature dealing with self-killing. Shakespeare's *Hamlet*, for example, deals profoundly with the choice of whether to continue living, and speculation about the afterlife. This is particularly true of the *to be or not to be* soliloquy.

More recently, there are those that say that suicide – once a crime – is morally unacceptable for whatever reason.

There are those who – in a secular world – might claim that as an autonomous individual you have the right to determine the time, place and manner of your death. This idea is leading to a more liberal approach to euthanasia in some European countries and, for example, in New Zealand. Not that it is that easy to decide when and how to die in these countries – not as easy as Ian McEwan's novel *Amsterdam* might lead you to believe. Voluntary euthanasia is probably still as difficult and bureaucratic to arrange in the Netherlands as adoption is in Britain.

The question of voluntary euthanasia belongs to the last circle of stakeholders – yourself – although most would agree that the next circle – close family – would still be relevant. Nonetheless, the overriding question is that of personal autonomy. However, this depends on the person concerned being fully aware of what they are doing, and on their conviction that the effects of their illness, perhaps depression and medical treatment, have not significantly impaired their judgement.

There is often a blurring of the distinction between euthanasia and suicide. In the Netherlands, for example, what is described as euthanasia is basically assisted suicide. Members of the Dutch Association of Voluntary Euthanasia complete the necessary paperwork with their doctor to cover the possibility of assisted suicide. When their illness has developed to the point where they feel their life is becoming unbearable, the doctor prescribes a bottle of poison, which they can keep with them. They can decide themselves when the moment has come to end their life. It is a private matter between patient and physician. This gives patients complete control over their life and death and represents total respect of personal autonomy.

In such cases, having the bottle of poison on their bedside cabinet as it were gives considerable comfort and peace of mind towards the end of life, and the feeling that they can decide when the time has come that life is not worth living, or that they have become too great a burden to others around them.

The doctor concerned has to satisfy himself that the patient knows absolutely what he is doing and that the decision hasn't been taken in a temporary fit of depression. There are safeguards. For example, apart from relevant stakeholders, such as family members, the doctor also has to discuss the case with another doctor before prescribing the means of ending life.

Suicide – self-killing – can be loosely divided between *giving* your life and *taking* your life. Even those who accept that giving your life for the sake of others is morally justifiable, might disapprove of you taking your life, especially when you take it to punish those you leave behind.

The classic case of someone giving their life is that of Captain Lawrence Oates, one of Scott's team on the famous, ill-fated expedition to the South Pole. When supplies were almost exhausted, Oates, already ill and a burden to the rest, gave his life by walking out into the blizzard, never to return.

However, most arguments against suicide are to do with *taking* life.

### Suicide – a free prescription

'*Has not every one ... the free disposal of his own life? And may he not lawfully employ that power with which nature has endowed him?*'

*British philosopher, David Hume, 'Of Suicide'.*

In an effort to sidestep easily refuted religious and social arguments, issues involving ending lives – such as suicide and euthanasia – are often attacked using the 'slippery slope' argument. For example, an argument against legalising euthanasia is that it will trigger an inexorable slide into the kind of thing SS Reichsführer, Heinrich Himmler had in mind for 'defective' people – enforced 'termination'. Similarly, in the case of suicide, it's not too difficult to imagine that if it's sanctioned in certain circumstances it might eventually become compulsory in those same circumstances.

Is suicide morally wrong when a person is both more a burden than a benefit to society and leading a life that has more personal and social *dis*value than value? If it is not morally wrong in those circumstances, it is only a tiny step away from being morally *right*. In that case it is only one step away from being morally *wrong not* to kill yourself in those same circumstances. This would be well on the way down the slippery slope.

It is worth looking at the issue through the minds of two very different philosophers – Britain's David Hume (1711-1776) and Albert Camus' compatriot, contemporary, and fellow philosopher, Jean-Paul Sartre. In addition to their specific interest in the morality of self-killing, Sartre and Hume are both interesting and relevant to ethical decision making in general because of the way they historically map the path away from recognition of divine authority, through societal authority to individual autonomy. It also presents an excellent opportunity to get to grips with Sartre's *existential philosophy*, which can offer inspiring guidance to making personal choices.

Sartre in particular inclines towards individual, personal responsibility for behaviour, rather than putting any store in theories of socially determined behaviour – or determinism, full stop, including the genetic variety.

**But first – David Hume**

The authority recognised as having the power to judge and make rules about suicide started with the Church, moved towards society and has now reached to the autonomy of the individual, leaving a large residue of those who believe in the Church or society, or both, or all three, as the sources of moral guidance on such matters. In Hume's time – the latter part of the *Age of Reason* – the shift (at least among intellectuals) would have already been towards societal, and even individual, authority, involving a rejection of the Church, and relying increasingly on 'reason'.

This would probably have brought Hume far enough to not want to reject the idea of compulsory suicide out of hand, because he would not have relied on any of the traditional rejections of suicide – a crime against God, a crime against other members of society, or against the self.

A 'deist' rather than a disciple of Church doctrine, he regarded God more as a prime mover and grand designer of the universe, than a day-to-day manager of the planet.

According to Hume, 'Since therefore the lives of men are for ever dependent on the general laws of matter and motion,' self-killing is no more a crime against the deity than any other alteration of the 'operations of nature', such as 'to divert the *Nile* or *Danube* from its course', without which 'they could not subsist a moment'.

Hume sums up his position with: 'Has not every one ... the free disposal of his own life? And may he not lawfully employ that power with which nature has endowed him?' He also points out that, 'There is not a single text of Scripture which prohibits it.'

In answer to the allegation that suicide is a crime against other members of society, Hume points out that, 'A man who retires from life, does no harm to society: He only ceases to do good.' And, even more relevant to the question: 'Suppose, that I am a burthen to it: Suppose, that my life hinders some person from being much more useful to the public. In such cases my resignation of life must not only be innocent but laudable.'

Hume also maintained that suicide can constitute a *duty to the self* in certain circumstances – '... age, sickness, or misfortune may ... make it [life] worse even than annihilation'.

Hume wouldn't have too much of a problem with suicide *per se*. But what about the slippery slope? Would he sanction a social rule making it a moral obligation in certain circumstances? Having rejected most of the traditional objections to suicide – as a breach of duty to God, society or self – he might be hard-pressed to find objections to its formal recommendation.

If he supported such a rule, it would be as an encouragement: '... both prudence and courage should engage us to rid ourselves at once of existence, when it becomes a burthen'. But the key lies in his insistence that 'Has not every one ... the free disposal of his own life?' This suggests a personal element – that suicide should not be morally condemned, but that at the same time there is no justification for saying that it *ought* to be done.

Hume's judgement of suicide is by reference mainly to its benefit or harm to the individual and society – a typically utilitarian point of view. When all stakeholders' interests are accounted for – those of the potential suicide, of relatives, perhaps doctors and nurses – and, on balance, the greatest benefit for the greatest number will result from the suicide.

Suicide is something done by the self to the self. Assuming selves can exist in isolation, it would seem to be essentially a private matter. This raises the question as to whether any general moral rules are applicable to it. Once all the mainstream objections have been cleared out of the way – sanctity of life, societal harm, and so forth – whether or not it would be acceptable (to Hume and Sartre) could boil down to the issue of personal autonomy. 'Has not every one ... the free disposal of his own life?' To morally disapprove of (or even outlaw) suicide, seems to reflect a lack of respect for the person concerned as an autonomous agent – a lack of respect for his deliberate choice of action, i.e. self-killing.

On the other hand, any rule that proposes making suicide a moral *ought* in certain circumstances, does exactly the same thing – it is disrespectful of autonomy.

### And now for Jean-Paul Sartre

The basis of Sartre's philosophy is that all individuals – comprising the 'Being-*for*-itself' (consciousness) and the 'Being-*in*-itself' (the body as an object) – have absolute responsibility for everything they are and do. How they apply that responsibility determines the degree of meaning their lives will have – the extent to which they come to terms with life in a world of meaningless objects and no independent values.

The realisation of the ultimate meaninglessness of life triggers 'existential anguish' – an uncomfortable experience that most people avoid by playing a role as though their actions were predestined, or morally determined, in order to escape ultimate responsibility for themselves. Such people behave as though they were things (Beings-in-itself); and, in Sartre's terms, act in 'bad faith'. 'Good faith', acknowledged by Sartre as never entirely attainable, comprises behaving in ways that involve no self-deception – by thinking and acting in ways true to oneself without even doing so self-consciously.

Would Sartre approve of suicide *per se*? And what would he make of fear of a social rule making suicide sometimes the right thing to do?

In Sartre's view, people's individual responsibility also includes whether to stay alive, or kill themselves – to choose whether to be a living individual or a dead one. The one problem with the second choice is that the essential *for*-itself component of the complete individual can no longer exist. All meanings are abruptly ended, because the sole source of those meanings – the conscious self – no longer exists.

And, even more disturbing, the *in*-itself part that remains (the body) could fall prey to re-identification (be given meanings) by those left behind – for example, rather than simply 'Jean-Paul deceased', he might become 'Jean-Paul the coward who couldn't take it', or 'Jean-Paul the martyr', etc., etc. Whatever he became he would no longer have any autonomous control over it.

What Sartre calls 'Seriousness' is bound up with 'bad faith' in the sense that it seeks an attitude that lies outside the individual – it looks for values in things, as if those values exist independently – for example, certain human 'virtues' – courage, selflessness, etc.; or certain values in objects, for example, of the kind used as ingredients of 'but is it art?' types of judgements – and projecting such values on others when standing in judgement of them.

When it comes to moral values, judging whether another individual has acted morally correctly would, too, involve Sartre's 'seriousness', because it would assume that the values used to judge are supra-individual, and therefore have a sort of independent existence. It seems almost as though moral rule making of any kind would be anathema to Sartre.

As for suicide specifically, any rule supporting it on the grounds that it would cause more happiness (less unhappiness) to the individual or the society in which he or she lives, would amount to an even greater act of 'bad faith'. This is because it would involve the sort of role-playing that stands in the way of self-realisation, and the 'authentic' choices that go with it. Suicide under the above rule would be self-killing as a 'good citizen', as a 'rule keeper' etc., rather than a freely chosen act aimed at enhancing one's mode of existence – even if that mode of existence is just simply 'choosing to be a suicide'.

**Sartre would probably consider suicide as a wasted opportunity, unless committed in 'good faith' where a person's overriding purpose in life is to end it. Such cases would be difficult to categorise, but that wouldn't matter – it matters only to the individual carrying it out. As for the moral rules relating to it, Sartre would want nothing to do with such rules in general, and would regard them as an encouragement to the ultimate act of 'bad faith'.**

# DEATH – FEAR OF THE UNKNOWN

It is fear of the unknown which

'... makes us rather bear those ills we have,
Than to fly to others that we know not of.
Thus conscience doth make cowards of us all.'

William Shakespeare, Hamlet, Act 3.

If there is little or no moral objection to self-killing, why don't more of us do it? It is still rare, even among those whose lives consist of appalling misery. It is often assumed that, no matter how awful life is, death is possibly an even worse alternative.

People who feel their life is no longer worth living, assuming national and religious laws allow it, would be confronted with the ultimate dilemma – to be or not to be. But, as we have seen above, genuine ethical choices depend on the personal freedom to make them. In most cases fear of death robs people of the freedom to make such a choice – *it doth make cowards of us all.*

But is it really reasonable to be afraid of dying? Is fear of your own death simply irrational, or can it be rationally justified. Or is it neither one nor the other?

'Fear' in this case refers to being afraid of the state of non-existence of the body, or the body and mind (soul, personality, memories, etc), rather than of the physical and emotional pain that can immediately precede death – fear of *death* rather than fear of *dying*.

*Reasons for fearing death include:*

- It has foreseeable 'bad' consequences.

- It is 'natural' to fear it, because such fears aid your survival, and, consequently, survival of the species.

- It is a stage on the path to another realm of life that might be worse than the present one.

*Reasons for **not** fearing death include:*

- It should be of no concern, because when you are dead you cannot experience it.

- It is something to be welcomed as bringing about the end to life's suffering.

- It is 'natural'.

- It is no more rational to fear your death than it is rational to regret the time before your birth.

- It is a stage on the path to another realm of life that is better than the present one.

*Death should be feared because of its foreseeable 'bad' consequences.*
From a utilitarian (consequentialist) standpoint, a natural death at the end of a fulfilled life could be judged 'good' in itself, but 'bad' in the light of its consequences for those left behind who might suffer the unhappiness of grief. Such foreseeable consequences of a good death after a good life could be sufficiently bad for the subject to fear that death.

*It is 'natural' to fear death, because such fears aid people's survival, and, consequently, survival of the species.*
British contemporary philosopher, Derek Parfit says humans are by their nature driven by the future, and that 'In giving us this bias, evolution denies us the best attitude to death'. As it stands, this attracts the criticism that it presupposes the validity of a scientific theory – the evolution theory – which cannot be relied upon to be *unfalsifiable*. But this does not undermine the core of the argument, which is that humans are oriented towards the future. This, of course, does not make a fear of death rational, but merely a genetically determined disposition.

German philosopher, Oswald Hanfling (1927-2005) makes the similar point that a *fear* of death '... may be attributed to the machinery of natural selection. A race of beings to whom life and death became indifferent would not survive very long'.

An alternative view, also appealing to determinism, would rely on the belief that the universe and the thinking beings that inhabit it are *rationally* structured by goals, purposes and projects they are themselves not even aware of. This is the view of some religions and Enlightenment deist thinking.

Albert Camus, without reference to unproven presuppositions such as 'natural selection' or 'evolution', says: 'The body's judgement is as good as the mind's and the body shrinks from annihilation. We get into the habit of living before acquiring the habit of thinking. In the race which daily hastens us towards death, the body maintains its irreparable lead'.

*Death should be of no concern, because when we are dead we cannot experience it.*
'Death ... is of no concern to us; for while we exist death is not present, and when death is present, we no longer exist,' says ancient Greek philosopher, Epicurus (341-270 BC). This is not particularly helpful, because it does not take account of the fact that something which will occur in the future ('is not present') nonetheless can be of concern in the present.

Also, we cannot know what it means to 'no longer exist' before we are dead. Meanwhile, while alive, all we can do is imagine it in all its negativity (lack of anything), or, possibly, an existence in Paradise or Hell. This might be sufficient to justify fearing death, even by those whose lives are thoroughly miserable.

*Death is something to be welcomed as bringing about the end to life's suffering.*
In the words of Epicurean philosopher, Lucretius (c.95-55 BC), 'One who is no longer cannot suffer'. The extent to which a person fears death is likely to depend to some extent on their quality of life. For someone like Prussian philosopher, Arthur Schopenhauer, who seems to have spent his entire conscious life in a state of depression, life might

not be worth living, and therefore death would be a splendid release from what Schopenhauer regarded as the vicious circle of long periods of desire each followed by only brief periods of boring satisfaction.

*Death is 'natural'.*
Lucretius aimed to establish that people are irrational to fear their future non-existence. 'Why do you weep and wail over death?', asks Lucretius. Life must have a natural end in the same way that enjoyments and sufferings within life have an end. Lucretius seems to be saying that death is natural, it is irrational to fear something that is natural, therefore, it is irrational to fear death.

First, this is helpful only in the case of a 'natural death', i.e. one that is expected and accounted for after having led a full life, rather than an 'unnatural', premature death. Secondly, it is also possible to reject the 'natural' death claim on the grounds that it amounts to a 'naturalistic fallacy' – it is a fallacy to assume that what is 'natural' is good or right, and therefore should not be feared. It was once thought natural to die at 30. To do so cannot be regarded as 'good', therefore 'natural' cannot be a sufficient condition of being 'good'.

*It is no more rational to fear one's death than it is rational to regret the time before one's birth.*
Lucretius also claimed that it is not rational to fear one's death any more than it is rational to regret the time before one's birth. His argument is: post-life non-existence and pre-life non-existence have in common their non-existence; because they both share non-existence, it is reasonable to regard the post-life state in the same way as the pre-life state; the pre-life state is not the object of regret, therefore, the post-life state is not the object of fear.

This argument seems to fail – not only because of its reliance on the common factor of 'non-existence' to regard post-life and pre-life states as the *same*, rather than merely *similar* – but because of an apparent conflation between 'fear' and 'regret'. This fails to take account of the fact that humans are driven by the future. The projects most people engage in are regarded as bringing about change (or 'progress') in the future. Even attempts to undo the consequences of past actions have to do with changing things in the future.

And, whilst 'regret' can apply to past events, 'fear' is an emotion that applies only to events that might happen in the future. It is impossible to be afraid of something happening in the past – even being afraid that some past event or action will come to light in the present is based on the fear of the future consequences of that discovery.

American philosopher Thomas Nagel (b. 1937) rejects the idea that even a natural death is normal. He claims, 'If we are to make sense of the view that to die is bad, it must be on the ground that life is good and death is the corresponding deprivation or loss, bad ... because of the desirability of what it removes'.

He concludes that because life, whatever its content, is good, death, which is a permanent non-existence, is a bad end. A bad end is something to be feared. Therefore permanent death may be something to be feared. His conclusion is rather hesitant because it can apply only 'to people whose lives are on balance good'.

And there are cases of people with satisfactory lives who still appear to be fearless of death. Keats, for example, wrote in his *Ode to a Nightingale*:

> ... and, for many a time
> I have been half in love with easeful death,
> ... Now more than ever seems it rich to die,
> To cease upon the midnight with no pain.

Keats (1795-1821) died in his mid twenties – a tragedy in Nagel's view – but Keats' poem seems to suggest the opposite.

*Death is merely a stage on the path to another realm of life (the view of most religions).*

Consideration of whether religious people would be rational to fear death is inconclusive. Those from the Judeo-Christian and Muslim traditions, for example, believe that death is a stage after which there is judgement, and then immortality in Heaven or Hell, perhaps with Heaven preceded by an uncomfortable spell in purgatory. They might fear death because they fear a guilty verdict on judgement day.

It is possible that there are those who are convinced that their life has been without sin, that, after death, they will pass on directly to Paradise, and that they have nothing to fear. There may also be those who believe, that despite being sinful, their deity's compassion will bring about a positive judgement. Again, they think they have no reason to fear death.

Many religious people believe in reincarnation. This is the belief that after death the human soul may live again in another human or animal. Basically, Hindus and Buddhists believe that how you reincarnate depends on your karma or past actions. Humans have the opportunity, through knowledge and devotion, to break the karmic chain and achieve final liberation from reincarnation, leaving them free to return to the creative force of the universe.

If this is not done in one life, it can be attempted in the next, and the form one takes in the next life – priest or pariah – depends on the quality of karma in the preceding life. Again, as in the case of those from the Judeo-Christian and Muslim traditions, the outcome of death is unpredictable, and could hold some nasty surprises. It could be heaven or it could be hell. It would, therefore, be perfectly rational to fear it.

**A tentative conclusion**

This brief consultation with a handful of influential philosophers suggests that there are several reasons why you might, or might not, fear death, and that many of these considerations, which often depend on individual personality, religious and/or philosophical beliefs, and quality of life, seem reasonable.

On the other hand, the fear of death and the desire to cling to life may have nothing to do with reasoning about anything. It may be to do with some inherited predisposition to fear death as a means to ensuring the survival of the human species.

Also, Albert Camus questions whether it is true to say that people regard death as a deprivation, and therefore as an evil to be feared? During World War Two, Camus saw people '... paradoxically getting killed for the ideas or illusions that gave them a reason for living – what is called a reason for living is also an excellent reason for dying'.

But many people share a common, psychological ground for fearing their own death – that it is unknown. It is something never before experienced by the person concerned, and there are no reliable reports of others' experiences of it.

Not that being 'unknown' is a sufficient condition for being 'feared'. Your next birthday presents are probably unknown to you, but fear wouldn't be appropriate. However, where 'the unknown' is whether a person will enjoy one pleasant experience rather than another pleasant experience might not be grounds for fear, this is not analogous with fear of death. The possibilities of nothingness, Paradise or Hell are not comparable with the possibilities of presents you do not want, and none of those you do. The stakes at death are so high, that the fact that the outcome is unknown will engender fear, and this is rationally justifiable.

Camus' point mentioned above about '... an excellent reason for dying' doesn't undermine this claim. The sort of heroism he hints at usually involves dying *despite* fear, not dying *without* fear.

However, in the case of death, there may be conditions in addition to being 'unknown' which, in combination, are *sufficient* to rationally justify fearing it.

The closest we can get to a conclusion seems to come via Oswald Hanfling who makes the point that – as in the case of painful childbirth – the fact that death (even painful death) is normal 'would mitigate the prospect of it to some extent'.

The analogy as it stands depends on regarding pain in childbirth as a necessary evil, and there is something counter-intuitive about the 'normality' of painful childbirth being compared to the 'normality' of death. Another problem is that, if the two are in any way comparable, it means that mothers will be better prepared to face their own mortality than men.

But the analogy is useful in comparing the *uncertainty* (unknown element) of the event, and the *lack of control* one has over it. These factors add to the justification of fearing it. Furthermore, it is analogous in the sense that childbirth, like death, is an experience that cannot be carried out by someone else on our behalf. It has to be faced up to personally.

**The conclusion is that it does seem to be perfectly reasonable to fear death because it is an event that is unknown, which has to be faced personally and over which you have no control.**

# PART IV

# 25

# FICTION – STRANGER THAN TRUTH

*One can't say how life is, how chance or fate deals with people, except by telling a tale.*

*Hannah Arendt, Philosopher, 1906-1975.*

Literature often describes the tension emanating from the pressure to do the right thing in difficult circumstances. Using fictional dilemmas in *Dilemma Training* is sometimes preferable to using real life ones, as it can take a long time to make the environment 'safe' from a group-dynamical point of view to enable participants to reveal their own dilemmas when they get too personal for comfort.

A thought-provoking philosophical justification for the use of literature over real life examples is given by Neo-Aristotelian philosopher Martha Nussbaum in *Love's Knowledge*. She writes:

> '(…) we have never lived enough. Our experience is, without fiction, too confined and too parochial. Literature extends it, making us reflect and feel about what might otherwise be too distant for feeling (…)'

and

> 'All living is interpreting; all action requires seeing the world as something. So in this sense no life is 'raw', and (as James and Proust insist) throughout our living we are, in a sense, makers of fictions. The point is that in the activity of literary imagining we are led to imagine and describe with greater precision, focusing our attention on each word, feeling each event more keenly – whereas much

*of actual life goes by without that heightened awareness, and is thus, in a certain sense, not fully or thoroughly lived.'*

Some of the following examples of ethical dilemmas found in literature are taken from *The Moral of the Story* by Australian philosophers, Peter and Renata Singer. This is essential reading for anyone interested in ethical decision making. Truth might be stranger than fiction, but the dilemmas featured in fiction are often more vivid and therefore more memorable.

The examples are put in order of the stakeholders' remoteness from the central character (see Chapter 2 for 'circles of stakeholders').

**The circles of stakeholders**

*You*

I should stand up for my civil rights and risk ill-treatment and death vs I should accept the abuse of my rights and enjoy a relatively safe existence for myself and my family.

*Invisible Man* by Ralph Ellison.

I should stand up for my rights but risk exclusion from my peer group vs I should accept the abuse of my rights for the sake of remaining within my peer group.

*Puberty Blues* by Kathy Lette and Gabrielle Carey.

I should accept 'hot' money or a bribe from someone who is corrupt but use it for a good cause vs I should reject the money as a matter of principle.

*Middlemarch* by George Eliot.

I should stand up for my sexual orientation but risk persecution vs I should repress my homosexuality for the sake of a safer existence.

*Giovanni's Room* by James Baldwin.

Rudyard Kipling's (1865-1936) inspirational and motivational poem *If* has long served many as a blueprint for personal integrity. Kipling has become unfashionable because of sexism in his works and his association with British Imperialism. Nonetheless *If* continues to be regarded as the possible basis for a personal ethos.

> *If you can keep your head when all about you*
> *Are losing theirs and blaming it on you,*
> *If you can trust yourself when all men doubt you,*
> *But make allowance for their doubting too;*
> *If you can wait and not be tired by waiting,*
> *Or being lied about, don't deal in lies,*
> *Or being hated, don't give way to hating,*
> *And yet don't look too good, nor talk too wise:*
> *If you can dream – and not make dreams your master,*
> *If you can think – and not make thoughts your aim;*
> *If you can meet with Triumph and Disaster*
> *And treat those two impostors just the same;*
> *If you can bear to hear the truth you've spoken*
> *Twisted by knaves to make a trap for fools,*
> *Or watch the things you gave your life to, broken,*
> *And stoop and build 'em up with worn-out tools:*
> *If you can make one heap of all your winnings*
> *And risk it all on one turn of pitch-and-toss,*
> *And lose, and start again at your beginnings*
> *And never breathe a word about your loss;*
> *If you can force your heart and nerve and sinew*
> *To serve your turn long after they are gone,*
> *And so hold on when there is nothing in you*
> *Except the Will which says to them: 'Hold on!'*
> *If you can talk with crowds and keep your virtue,*
> *Or walk with kings – nor lose the common touch,*
> *If neither foes nor loving friends can hurt you,*

*If all men count with you, but none too much;*
*If you can fill the unforgiving minute*
*With sixty seconds' worth of distance run,*
*Yours is the Earth and everything that's in it,*
*And – which is more – you'll be a Man, my son!*

### Your partner

Carrie's Choice: Kipling's wife Carrie had her own terrible choice. Soon after their arrival in New York, Rudyard Kipling and his daughter Josephine fell seriously ill. Kipling's wife Carrie was weak with illness and had finally to decide to look after one of them. She didn't have the strength to care for both. She chose to look after her husband, and Josephine died. How she reached this decision is not known.

### Your Children

I should put my own child's life in danger to save the lives of many strangers vs I should save my own child at the expense of the lives of many strangers.

*An Unnatural Mother* by Charlotte Perkins Gilman.

I should sacrifice my time and attention for my own children for the sake of taking time to work to help many more children in need vs I should spend more time on my own children that could have been spent on helping many more children in need.

*Bleak House* by Charles Dickens.

I should become the lover of the man I love vs I should become the lover of the man who can best save my children.

*Dr Zhivago* by Boris Pasterak.

I should preserve my family and child and deny my love for

another vs I should elope with the one I love and sacrifice my family and child.

*Anna Karenina* by Leo Tolstoy.

## Your siblings

I should surrender my virginity and honour to save the life of my brother (sister) vs I should maintain my virginity and honour on principle even though it will be at the cost of my sister's (brother's) life.

*Measure for Measure* by William Shakespeare.

## Your parents

I should do my duty towards my parents at the expense of my own family vs I should do my duty towards my own family at the expense of my parents.

*The Peace of Utrecht* by Alice Munro.

## Others

I should lie to betray one person to save the lives of many others vs I should tell the truth to save one person at the expense of many.

*The Crucible* by Arthur Miller.

## The Law

I should break the law and assist someone to die who wants to die vs I should obey the law and allow someone to live and suffer against their wishes.

*Whose Life is it Anyway?* by Brian Clark and *Moral Hazard* by Kate Jennings.

## Integrity and Betrayal

*Innocence always calls mutely for protection, when we would be so much wiser to guard ourselves against it: innocence is like a dumb leper who has lost his bell, wandering the world meaning no harm.*

*Graham Greene, The Quiet American, 1955.*

Graham Greene's *The Quiet American*, a prophetic book about the disastrous consequences of America's 'well-intentioned' intervention abroad, focuses sharply on two paradoxes of ethical action which make ethical choices so difficult – when apparent 'integrity' leads to bad consequences; when bad behaviour – in this case, betrayal – can limit further damage. This 'betrayal' causes a murder.

Based around the story of a love triangle between a naive American intelligence agent, a world-weary British journalist, and a young Vietnamese girl, the book is about how blind adherence to clean-cut ideologies can smother the ability to take account of human consequences – the rights of other stakeholders – and how the vice of betrayal translated into the virtue of saving lives.

## Poetry in emotion

*'A man, to be greatly good, must imagine intensely and comprehensively; he must put himself in the place of another and many others; the pains and pleasures of his species must become his own.'*

*Percy Bysshe Shelley (1792-1822), A Defence of Poetry.*

Unable to believe in the sort of God who intervened in world events, 19th century Romantic poet, Shelley, together with other thinkers at the time, believed that what he termed 'civilised imagination' was essential to the kind of empathy necessary to making ethical decisions that took proper account of the interests of other people affected by them. He firmly maintained that poetry helps to build that kind of imagination.

On the other hand, it could be argued that people like Sophie were the victim of imagination. It took a rich imagination to create Auschwitz. The key here is Shelley's phrase *'civilised imagination'*.

'Disinterested benevolence is the product of a civilised imagination,' he wrote in his essay *A Treatise on Morals*. Later, in his essay *A Defence of Poetry*, he wrote: 'The great instrument of moral good is the imagination ... Poetry strengthens that faculty which is the organ of the moral nature of man, in the same manner that exercise strengthens a limb.'

**And this is important. It's not enough to know how to act ethically. It has meaning only when acting ethically at all times and in all circumstances becomes a habit.**

# 26

# A BRIEF HISTORY

# OF ETHICAL DECISION MAKING

*Is something right because the Gods command it, or do they command it because it's right?*

*Socrates, c.470-399 BC.*

Socrates 470-399 BC

Morality is under the spotlight. Standards are widely perceived to be declining rapidly, leaving a 'moral vacuum'.

The postwar trend, especially in the West, has been to chisel away at traditional morality, and establish a new morality based on individual judgement. Re-establishment of values and standards is still taking place. Since the end of the 1960s traditional authorities such as the Church, parents and teachers have been challenged or completely rejected as leaders on moral issues. The breakup of traditional authority and the democratisation of moral culture have given everyone the space to make up their own minds.

This should lead to more tolerance and mutual respect. But there are many obstacles. It's not just a matter of who says how to act that is changed, the idea of what is appropriate action has also changed.

The perceived decline in traditional moral authority has gone hand in hand with an increase in legal authority in a much more complex society. But laws often create even more problems. In practice they are often a poor substitute for the loss of traditional authority. They are nearly always *re*active rather than *pro*active, and can undermine and discourage attempts to face up to personal moral responsibility.

There might be truth in the 'moral vacuum' argument, although even when Church authority was at its most influential, people still faced the sort of ethical dilemmas they face today.

This chapter aims to place ethical decision making in an historical context. It demonstrates that the return to personal responsibility is not a current fad. It has been a gradual one over several hundred years, and that the so-called 'moral vacuum' is not the result of two world wars, abandonment of military service or the myriad of other 20th century social changes that have been blamed for it, but is the product of an evolution that dates back to the Renaissance. This evolution is reflected in philosophy, art, and literature.

The decline in the authority of the Church too is not new. Ideas about humans being at the centre of the universe have been around for a few hundred years. What *is* new is that these ideas have finally filtered down through most strata of society. While *avant-garde* thinkers have long been preoccupied with post-modernism, Enlightenment modernism has finally arrived for the masses.

## From Greeks to PC fundamentalism

At the time of Christ, the West and the Middle East were part of the Roman Empire where Greek slaves employed as tutors taught the works of ancient Greek philosophers such as Plato and Aristotle. In the mid-400s AD the West and East split after the empire's collapse. The West was ruled by 'barbarians'. The East, including Alexandria in Egypt, became a seat of learning, ruled by Arabs.

It wasn't until the 11th century that the Crusades put the West back in touch with the East. The Crusaders discovered Latin and Syriac translations of Greek texts of ancient scholars. Aristotle was rediscovered. This triggered a western interest in Greek sciences that was promptly stamped on by the Holy Roman Church. Prevailing theology considered not 'nature' but 'salvation' to be of paramount importance.

This tension between 'faith' and 'reason' was finally resolved by Christian theologian Thomas Aquinas (1225-1274). He managed to reconcile Christianity with rational explanations of the natural world, by assimilating Aristotelian philosophy with Christian thought. He harnessed rationality to the service of Christianity – rationality being common to all people of any religion. However, dismantling one stone wall led to the erection of another. Aristotle gained unassailable authority, which stifled any further enquiry.

One interesting argument for the Church's support of Aristotle was based on its belief in the 'decay of nature' – that nature had declined since the perfection of God's original creation. Therefore the Ancients' knowledge must be superior to that of contemporaries. As a result, ancient knowledge was studiously preserved by Scholastics in mediaeval universities.

Aristotle said the earth is motionless and at the centre of the cosmos. The heavenly bodies move around it in concentric spheres each governed by its own divine spirit. For the Christian, these spirits were angels. Beyond the outermost sphere was the realm of God – the Unmoved Mover. God caused all motion in the cosmos, by the desire all things had for God.

Yet pure observation by philosophers such as Copernicus in the 16th century proved that the sun is the centre of our cosmos. This led to a fierce attack by the Church, in which *avant-garde* thinkers such as Copernicus and Galileo nearly burned at the stake – the fate of Italian philosopher Giordano Bruno and many others. It took 400 years until the end of the 20th century before the Roman Catholic Church grudgingly admitted that Galileo had been right in supporting the theories of Copernicus.

Yet, despite the Church's fierce opposition, the Renaissance continued to flourish with the study of Man and Nature. The 15th century saw the collapse of mediaeval feudal social order, and to a large extent the collapse of Aristotelianism. The invention of the printing press enabled dissemination of new ideas.

Voyages of discovery revealed Aristotle's errors and helped undermine the authority of the Ancient Greek philosophers upon which the Church rested so heavily.

Then, in the 16th century, Augustinian monk Martin Luther nailed a statement of 99 theses attacking papal indulgences to a church door in Wittenburg, Germany. Luther said the only interpretation scripture required was in the light of *individual* conscience.

Then came Francis Bacon with his investigation of nature by accumulation of fact, and gradually one authority was replaced by another – Science. Not that these developments did away with God. Philosophers simply set their faces against the authority of the Church. Most still believed in a deity – a creator and prime mover of the universe – even Enlightenment philosophers such as Voltaire, who had called for annihilation of the Church – '*Écrasez l'Infâme!*'.

However, the new authority, science, still needs to be treated with a healthy dose of scepticism, and in no way undermines the caveat *think for yourself!* There have been many revolutions in physics. Each new theory has sprung up on the demolished foundations of the theory preceding it, for example the theories of Newton and Einstein. It seems probable that future scientific revolutions will discredit present ideas.

Nonetheless, science can discover the workings of the natural world, even if it never completely uncovers the principles behind it. The possibility that the match between theory and fact will never be perfect doesn't mean the practice of science is futile. Perhaps humans just have to accept that they are not cut out to formulate a complete and final theory of the physical world.

However, people do seem to need beliefs to replace 'religion', and there is the temptation to commit themselves to alternative 'religions' such as New Ageism and multifarious other 'isms' and gurus. Even 'political correctness' has become an external authority. Those determined to be seen to be 'PC', or scared not to be, often devote unswerving and unquestioning obedience to it, rather than thinking each issue through for themselves.

**Think for yourself! A catchphrase with a long history**

Two mainstream philosophical positions in the 18th century Enlightenment period were rationalism and empiricism. A subject of enquiry was neutral – independent of history, prejudice, superstition, and God. This idea that knowledge is based purely on sense experience reflects the ideas of philosophers such as Locke, Berkeley, and Hume.

This was also reflected in art. For example, French artist Chardin's extreme regard for truth, and his faithful and exact imitation of nature, particularly in a modest, domestic scene, was typically 'Enlightenment'; following the Dutch and Flemish painters' depiction of lowly, everyday secular scenes oozing moral decency, in place of grand religious ones.

Like 'Renaissance' and 'Middle Ages', the term 'Enlightenment' is a chronological abstraction used to isolate one historical period from another. Yet the period was characterised as much by its cultural and philosophical variety, as by its homogeneity.

The one common factor was the period's continued development of secular beings, intent on this-worldly affairs. Empiricism – verifying facts through personal experience, rather than through ideas or authorities – arose from the need to understand a secular universe in the hands of mere mortals, without reference to ancient scholarly texts, or medieval consultation of God's word. The need for a change in the concept of authority was embodied in a turning away from the Church and authority in general.

Scottish sceptic, David Hume (1711-1776) exploded one after another all the basic concepts in terms of which western man had interpreted their experience of the universe since the ancient Greeks.

And all this was happening almost 300 years ago.

Even empiricism, the cornerstone of the Enlightenment ethos, was consolidated but not new. It had already been reflected in the realistic writings of Chaucer, in 15th century world exploration, and in the problems of perspective occupying the minds of 15th century painters such as Leonardo da Vinci. The father of the empiricists, the Englishman Francis Bacon, was born in 1561. His monastic namesake Roger Bacon (1214-1294) was conducting scientific experiments into optics as early as 1240.

Another passionate believer in the requirement for personal judgement and responsibility was 19th century philosopher and social reformer, John Stuart Mill (see chapter 6). The *Greatest Happiness Principle* of his fellow utilitarians, for all its shortcomings as a guide to ethical action, does allow a defence of civil liberties that avoids the kind of control and compulsion that can occur when liberty is based on rights alone; and that can lead to repression of opinion.

In his book *On Liberty* he argues passionately against conformity that is based on external authority. The only freedom 'which deserves the name is that of pursuing our own good in our own way, so long as we do not attempt to deprive others or impede their efforts to obtain it. Each is the proper guardian of his own health, whether bodily or mental and spiritual'.

Mill points out that people who are in a position to tell you what to do or think are fallible – and that includes teachers. You end up thinking things are *certain*, just because *they* think they are certain.

**The need for that sense of personal responsibility is now stronger than ever. In the advent of the rise of religious fundamentalism East and West, the need to 'think for yourself' has never been greater. When you stop doubting, you stop thinking – a sure route to error.**

## Religion – what has God got to do with it?

*Turning and turning in the widening gyre*
*The falcon cannot hear the falconer;*
*Things fall apart; the centre cannot hold;*
*Mere anarchy is loosed upon the world,*
*The blood-dimmed tide is loosed, and everywhere*
*The ceremony of innocence is drowned;*
*The best lack all conviction, while the worst*
*Are full of passionate intensity.*
*Surely some revelation is at hand;*
*Surely the Second Coming is at hand.*
*The Second Coming! Hardly are those words out*
*When a vast image out of Spiritus Mundi*
*Troubles my sight: somewhere in the sands of the desert*
*A shape with lion body and the head of a man,*
*A gaze blank and pitiless as the sun,*
*Is moving its slow thighs, while all about it*
*Reel shadows of the indignant desert birds.*
*The darkness drops again; but now I know*
*That twenty centuries of stony sleep*
*Were vexed to nightmare by a rocking cradle,*
*And what rough beast, its hour come round at last,*
*Slouches towards Bethlehem to be born?*

*The Second Coming, William Butler Yeats, 1865-1939.*

Karl Marx called religion 'opium for the people' – offering pipe dreams and illusions that stand in the way of facing up to reality. Religions seem to offer certainties. Yet the reality is that certainty itself is an illusion. It has been claimed that religious belief reflects society's immaturity and avoidance of personal responsibility.

Another point to bear in mind is that no one religious doctrine has any more claim to moral authority than any other. The doctrines of many religions have diverted so wildly from the teaching of their original founders, whether to satisfy greed for power or merely to 'move with the times', that they have lost all credibility as a basis for ethical decision making. Also, it offers little guidance for the myriad of everyday decisions.

No matter what *The Bible*, *The Koran* or any other religious scripture prescribes, if it doesn't add up and it doesn't feel right – if you can't answer 'yes' to the question 'is what I am doing morally correct?' – then you have to treat it with scepticism.

That is not to say that because you reject its moral authority that you have to reject the whole religion. This chapter treats 'religion' mainly as meaning 'the Church and religious doctrine' rather than 'belief in God' and 'spiritual experience'.

## The Church under attack – deism

Before the French Revolution at the end of the 18th century, the Enlightenment period embodied a spirited sense of experimentation and criticism. And although the 18th century French philosophers (*philosophes*) were always arguing about almost everything, at least two points unified them – rationality and humanism.

Religious doctrine was an obvious target. It embodied a system of worship with strict rules, dogma, and mysticism that appeared to many as irrational to the point of superstition. Men and women of reason rejected anything they could not justify rationally, and this usually included religious dogma. The manner in which they rejected it varied from the vicious and melodramatic, through the more tender and bemused, to one full of scientific certainty.

The French philosophers were viewed with acute suspicion both by State and Church as threats to religion and therefore to morality. Most supported deism in which God's role is limited to being the cause of the cause/effect laws which govern the nature of the universe, but he no longer supervises it.

Influenced by Newton's physics and its evidence of the 'reasonableness' of the universe, the deists saw the universe as a huge machine, operating according to natural laws. Reason suggests this machine must have a prime mover – and most accepted that this must be God. Because his works are visible for all to appreciate – for example, the rising and setting of the sun – there was no need for churches, scriptures and sacraments. All one needed was reason and a conscience for guidance.

For a down-to-earth guide to moral behaviour the philosophers looked back to the Roman Augustan age, when a moral code already existed that appeared more rational and humanistic than anything Christianity had produced – the *Humanitas*, a code that had evolved in a society of pagans, and had nothing to do with God.

The French philosophers – together with contemporaries in Britain such as David Hume and the poet Alexander Pope – tried to expose as nonsense, irrational superstition and doctrines, such as belief in miracles. They were humanist, placing wo/man at the centre of the universe, but still recognising God as the prime mover. The world had been created by God, but was now clearly in the hands of humanity, a humanity which, it was believed, possessed common feelings, aspirations, and sentiments, such as pursuit of happiness, but above all, reason.

**The age of miracles *is* dead**

The immeasurably influential Scottish philosopher David Hume (1711-1776) revered Isaac Newton's physical laws, and set out to define human nature in the same rational terms. He not only devastatingly demonstrated the irrationality of religious doctrine, but went one step further to claim sceptically that even the power of reason and experience has its limitations as a path to knowledge.

One obvious subject at which he aimed his scepticism was

the Church's claim that reports of Jesus' miracles were true.

'No testimony is sufficient to establish a miracle, unless the testimony be of such a kind, that its falsehood would be more miraculous, than the fact, which it endeavours to establish ...' said Hume in 'Of Miracles' in his *An Enquiry Concerning Human Understanding*.

Hume is highly sceptical about whether testimony adequate to support a miracle has ever been recorded. He goes on to consider a number of cases where a miracle has been claimed, and concludes that 'no testimony for any kind of miracle has ever amounted to a probability, much less to a proof'.

A tough-minded sceptic, Hume laboured under none of the piety or mysticism of philosophers before him. His open-mindedness cleared the path to conclusions to which he felt irresistibly drawn by the force of logic; rather than being sidetracked by false belief and superstition. He accepted only arguments based on experience, and was dismissive of any attempts at *a priori* knowledge of the world beyond the limited area of geometry.

The question of religion was no exception. Logically it boils down to two fundamental questions – can God's existence be proved? And can anything be known about his nature? If the answers to either or both are 'no', then the basis for traditional theology can no longer be sustained.

He had already defined religion as something founded on *faith*, not on reason. Therefore belief in religious truth was unreasonable. Determined unreasonableness, when translated into action, descends into the dark realms of superstition and 'enthusiasm' – what today would be called 'fundamentalism' – the manifestations of which Hume, and many other Enlightenment philosophers such as Voltaire, were keen to attack in all forms.

But 'Of Miracles' isn't just about miracles, nor even just about religion. It serves as a revealing example that for Hume there were no sacred cows – not even God and *The Bible* – which were beyond the reach of his relentless insistence that knowledge about anything can be derived from experience only; and that 'knowledge' derived from any other source was no more than mere superstition.

The decline in the authority of the Church has a long history. With some exceptions, this decline did not reflect a decline in the belief in God, but in the belief that the Church could explain the workings of the universe, or should be the moral authority to guide ethical action. Furthermore, it does not reject the other benefits associated with religious worship common to most religions East and West, which fulfil a deep human need for ritual, a sense of otherworldliness, and for spirituality.

**Nonetheless, personal responsibility is paramount. In the words of Robert Pirsig, author of *Zen and the Art of Motorcycle Maintenance*, 'The only Zen you will find on the tops of mountains is the Zen you bring up there'.**

# THE LAST WORD

If you have got this far, you have come a very long way since embarking on the *Preface*. You have met the concept of ethical decision making and the moral theories underpinning it. You have also been introduced to some of the areas of activity where training in ethical decision making has been successfully applied.

Part III led you through the ethical dilemmas of various life and death issues, and Part IV presented a historical background to the idea that people have a right to think for themselves, rather than having to refer to authorities such as religious doctrine.

This book has hopefully given you the opportunity to think about the ways in which the choices you make matter to yourself and others.

Before you put it back on the shelf, it is worth reminding yourself of two key elements involved in making effective decisions when faced with choosing between two or more apparently right courses of action.

One is the need to think for yourself. Another is that ethical behaviour rests largely on tolerance and empathy for others, and respect for their beliefs, desires and ways of life. It allows for the interests and rights of others, and demands that you carefully and honestly establish who these 'others' are. The *burning house thought experiment* is extremely useful in deciding how to rank your priorities.

Differences, real and perceived, can provoke conflict. There appears to be no end to the intolerance people show towards those who are in some way different. Yet, compared with the very few differences, the similarities between people of different races and creeds, and even between humans and higher animals, are vast.

Some politicians deliberately use ethnic differences to whip up fear and aggression against people of different races or religions. They often point to such differences in the context of survival – as a battle for jobs, land, homes and security. Concentration on differences rather than commonalities, and a failure to appreciate the rights of different stakeholders affected by choices of behaviour has led to appalling destruction and cruelty – among others in Nazi Germany, America's Deep South, South Africa's *apartheid* period, Israel/Palestine, the former Yugoslavia, Rwanda and Darfur.

It is essential to recognise the connection between personal behaviour and international aggression. Wars are started by people. They are nearly always founded on a sense of ethnic or religious difference, feelings of superiority or fears about 'survival', and more importantly, a lack of consideration for the rights and wishes of those affected by these conflicts.

It makes much more sense to focus on human commonalities – on what unites, rather than separates, this planet's inhabitants.

**If the world is to become a more peaceful place, it is vital that ethical decision making becomes an integral part of life for all of us. The ability personally to make the right ethical decisions in difficult circumstances and under pressure, taking account of all concerned, is a necessary ingredient for a good life – a flourishing, decent life, for whomever, wherever, whenever.**

# REFERENCES & FURTHER READING

## Ethics

| | |
|---|---|
| Aristotle | *The Polities* |
| Hanfling, Oswald | *The Quest for Meaning* |
| Harvey, Peter | *An Introduction to Buddhism* |
| Hursthouse, Rosalind | *Beginning Lives* |
| Mackie, J L | *Ethics: Inventing Right and Wrong* |
| Mill, John Stuart | *Nature* |
| Mill, John Stuart | *On Liberty* |
| Murris, Karin | *Six Steps to Better Decisions* |
| Murris, Karin & Haynes, Joanna | *Storywise – Thinking through Stories* |
| Nussbaum, Martha | *Love's Knowledge* |
| Nuttall, Jon | *Moral Questions: An Introduction to Ethics* |
| Phillips, D Z | *Death and Immortality* |
| Pirsig, Robert | *Zen and the Art of Motorcycle Maintenance* |
| | *Lila* |
| Rousseau, Jean-Jacques | *Discourse of the Origin of Inequality* |
| Singer, Peter | *Applied Ethics* |
| Straughan, Roger | *Can We Teach Children to be Good?* |
| Taylor, Richard | 'The Singer Revolution'; In: *Philosophy Now*, Issue 28 |
| Warburton, Nigel | *Philosophy: the Basics* |

## Argument

| | |
|---|---|
| Brink-Budgen, Roy van den | *Critical Thinking for AS Level* |
| Thouless, Robert H | *Straight and Crooked Thinking* |
| Warburton, Nigel | *Thinking from A to Z* |

## Education
## Dilemmas in Picture Books

### From KeyStage 1

| | |
|---|---|
| Coleman, Michael | *Lazy Ozzie* |
| Foreman, Michael | *Dinosaurs and All the Rubbish* |

| | |
|---|---|
| Grey, Mini | *Biscuit bear* |
| McKee, David | *Not Now Bernard* |
| | *Tusk Tusk* |
| Murphy, Jill | *The Last Noo-Noo* |
| Sendak, Maurice | *Where The Wild Things Are,* |
| Velthuys, Max | *Frog and The Birdsong* |
| | *Frog and The Stranger etc* |
| Wagner, Jenny & | |
| Brooks Ron | *John Brown, Rose and the Midnight Cat* |

## From Keystage 2

| | |
|---|---|
| Allsburgh, Chris van | *The Sweetest Fig* |
| Baker, Jeannie | *Home in the Sky* |
| Browne, Anthony | *The Tunnel* |
| | *The Visitors Who Came to Stay* |
| | *Zoo* |
| Gaiman, Neil & | |
| McKean, Dave | *The Day I Swapped my Dad for Two Goldfish* |
| Gerstein, Mordicai | *The Mountains of Tibet* |
| Innocenti, Roberto & | |
| McEwan, Ian | *Rose Blanche* |
| | *Erika's Story* |
| Maddern, Eric & | |
| Hess, Paul | *Death in a Nut* |
| Morrison, Toni with | |
| Morrison, Slade & | |
| Lemaitre, Pascal | *Who's got game?* |
| | *Poppy or the Snake* |
| Paola, Tomie de | *Strega Nona* |
| Tan, Shaun | *The Rabbits* |
| Thompson, Colin | *How To Live Forever* |
| Ungerer, Tomi | *The Beast of Monsieur Racine* |
| | *The Three Robbers* |

## Keystages 3 and 4

Singer, Peter & Renate    *The Moral of the Story*

## Specially made collections for moral education (from Key stage 2)

Cohen, Martin             *Ethical Dilemmas*
Fisher, Robert            *Values for Thinking*

## General

Browne, Anthony           *The Retreat of Reason: Public Correctness and the Corruption of Public Debate in Modern Britain*

Bureau Integriteit at     *Training Morele oordeelsvorming;*
Amsterdam Council         *Handleiding voor trainers*
Cohen, Martin             *Ethical Dilemmas*
Donaldson, Margaret       *Children's Minds*
Haynes, Joanna            *Children as Philosophers*
                          What should I do? In:*Teaching Thinking & Creativity*. Issue 15
Kelly, A.V.               *Education and Democracy*
Kidder, Rushworth         *How Good People Make Tough Choices*
Lakoff, George &
 Johnson, Mark            *Philosophy in the Flesh; the Embodied Mind and its Challenge to Western Thought*
Lipman, Matthew           *Philosophy Goes To School*
Luijk, Henk van           *Integer en verantwoord in Beroep and Bedrijf*

Matthews, Gareth          *The Philosophy of Childhood*
Murris, Karin             Can Children Do Philosophy? In: *Journal of Philosophy of Education*, Vol. 34, Issue 2.

Murris, Karin             Making School a Better Place.In: *Teaching Thinking & Creativity*. Issue 14

Murris, Karin &
 Haynes, Joanna           *StoryWise: Thinking through Stories*
Nussbaum, Martha          *Love's Knowledge; Essays on Philosophy and Literature*

| | |
|---|---|
| Taylor, Charles | *The Ethics of Authenticity* |

**Euthanasia**

| | |
|---|---|
| Beauchamp &<br>  Childress | *Principles of Biomedical Ethics* |
| Campbell, Robert &<br>  Di Collinson | *Ending Lives* |
| McEwan, Ian | *Amsterdam* |

**Suicide**

| | |
|---|---|
| Camus, Albert | *The Myth of Sisyphus* |
| Hanfling, Oswald | *Life and Meaning* |
| Hume, David | *Of Suicide* |
| Lucretius | *On the Nature of the Universe* |
| Nagel, Thomas | *Death* |
| Parfit, Derek | *Reasons and Person* |
| Sartre, Jean-Paul | *Being and Nothingness* |
| Shakespeare, William | *Hamlet* |
| Singer, Peter | *Applied Ethics* |

**Religion**

| | |
|---|---|
| d'Holbach, Baron | *Le Système de la Nature* |
| Helvétius, Claude | *De l'esprit* |
| Hume, David | *An Enquiry Concerning Human*<br>*Understanding* |
| Leclerc, Georges-Louis<br>  Comte de Buffon | *L'Histoire Naturelle* |
| Otto, Rudolf | *Das Heilige* |
| Rousseau,<br>  Jean-Jacques | *Emile* |

**Literature**

| | |
|---|---|
| Baldwin, James | *Giovanni's Room* |
| Carré, John le | *The Constant Gardener*<br>*Absolute Friends* |
| Clark, Brian | *Whose Life is it Anyway?* |
| Dickens, Charles | *Bleak House* |
| Eliot, George | *Middlemarch* |
| Ellison, Ralph | *Invisible Man* |

| | |
|---|---|
| Gilman, Charlotte Perkins | *An Unnatural Mother* |
| Greene, Graham | *The Third Man* |
| | *The Quiet American* |
| Jennings, Kate | *Moral Hazard* |
| Lette, Kathy and Carey, Gabrielle | *Puberty Blues* |
| Miller, Arthur | *The Crucible* |
| Munro, Alice | *The Peace of Utrecht* |
| Pastenak, Boris | *Dr Zhivago* |
| Shakespeare, William | *Measure for Measure* |
| Singer, Peter & Renata | *The Moral of the Story* |
| Styron, William | *Sophie's Choice* |
| Tolstoy, Leo | *Anna Karenina* |

**Further information**

Please see www.amiright.co.uk for further information.